UGLY CHILD

KATE SKYLARK as SIOBHAN LENNON

Ugly Child

My Own True Story of Child Abuse and the
Fight for Survival

Disclaimer

This book is based on true events.

The names of people and places have been changed to protect the innocent.

COVER PHOTOGRAPH IS POSED BY A MODEL AND IS USED FOR ILLUSTRATIVE PURPOSES ONLY.

For every book sold, a donation will be made to the National Society for the Prevention of Cruelty to Children (NSPCC).

CONTENTS

CHAPTER 1
A Note from Kate

My real name is not Kate Skylark. I cannot reveal my true surname for obvious reasons; but I will tell you my true first name. My first name is Siobhan. This lovely Irish name has been the cause of such misery to me over the years. Because being a 'Siobhan', rather than an Emma or a Louise or a Sarah or a Nicola, set me apart as different right from the very beginning.

When writing this book it rather sadly felt quite lovely to become a 'Kate'. Kate is not different or unusual. Everyone has heard it before. Everyone can spell it. Kate is a solid, sensible, non-threatening name. Kate is confident and sure of herself.

Kate is *everyone's* friend.

I am a victim of childhood sexual abuse and I also co-write books to enable others to tell their abuse stories. You may have read *Dirty Little Dog* and *Daddy's Wicked Parties,* both of which I wrote in collaboration with the victims of those stories. Writing these books has been a sort of catharsis for me. I especially like the stories that have some element of revenge, of retribution. I like to be constantly reminded that good always overcomes evil. And this is why I continue to read stories of child abuse and to help others to tell their stories.

But for some time now, I have been putting off the inevitable. Although I knew it would eventually have to come out, for some time I have resisted telling my own story. I fully realise that my experiences of abuse are nothing like as bad as some of those I have read, or in those books I have helped write. Lucy and Sophie, the two little girls in the books I mentioned above, suffered far worse abuse than I ever did. I salute those girls, now women, for having the courage, first to turn their lives around, and second for having the strength to tell their stories. And their courage has given me the push I needed. After all, if they can do it with stories far worse than mine, what excuse can I possibly have for continuing to hide away?

But there is something quite different about my story. It is quite unlike any of those I have read, or those I have helped to write. Because my abuser was not my father, my teacher, or a random stranger. Not my uncle or stepdad, not a friend of the family. My abuser was altogether more unexpected than that.

CHAPTER 2

I was never a beautiful child. Or so I overheard my own grandmother saying once. She hadn't realised I was standing at the door while she and my auntie were looking over photos of my sister and me. 'Michaela was such a pretty baby, but Siobhan was never a beautiful child,' she said sadly.

It was not a nice thing to say. But my grandmother was right. I have the photos to prove it. This is not the story of an adorable, angelic, doll-like little girl, with long blonde ringlets and huge blue eyes, like my sister, Michaela. This is the story of a large, gangly, awkward girl with fuzzy brown hair and rather greasy skin. I was not just large; I was also tall, really tall from an early age. I had to wear uniform for girls three years older than me. I felt, from early childhood, like an ugly, hulking, clunking, huge mass of a child. I was the one chosen to help carry things, to move chairs and lift tables. I never got to be Mary in the school nativity. I always got the part of the tree.

I was never popular with other children. You see, I was one of those odd ones, what they now call 'weirdos'. Back when I was at school, 'weirdo' was not a term widely used. But there were plenty of others. Spaz, Flid, Joey, Mong, Zitty, Sod, and one that started in very early childhood, one that was right there with my earliest memories.

Freak.

But there was more. When I was born, mine was a breach birth and I came out the wrong way around and upside down. My mother had a very traumatic labour and I missed out on the required amount of oxygen. Not much, but just enough to have a very tiny effect on me. I was left with a very, very mild case of cerebral palsy, or spasticity as it was still often called back then. Most of the time this mild disability was barely noticeable. Most onlookers would never assume I was anything but one hundred per cent normal. But what my very mild case of spasticity did to me was devastating. It made me look, move and speak *ever so slightly differently.* And those who were a bit different didn't have an easy time of it.

One hand was ever so slightly turned inward. My legs a little loose, as if they weren't properly attached at the hip. My head didn't have the quick, flirty movements of the other girls, but moved more slowly, deliberately. My eyes opened a little too wide, my speech was a little stilted, like I was adding in extra consonants.

All this combined to give the impression, not of a disabled child, but of a weird child, an odd child, a clumsy, awkward, insufferably gauche child. I remember seeing a troupe of chimpanzees on television and the way they attacked a cuddly toy introduced into their cage. They screamed and ran around shouting, throwing stones at the odd thing. I have also seen a whole group of mallard ducks in a pond attack the one white duck, ganging up on it because it didn't fit in. That's how I felt, most of the time. And that is how I was, I was the odd thing – the irritatingly, maddeningly different thing. Not quite disabled enough to inspire pity or condescension, and not normal enough to love. I simply wasn't easy to *like*. I was just a bit spooky, a bit bewildering, a bit wrong: a bit *weird*.

I often used to think that if only I had been a bit worse, a bit more disabled – if I had needed a stick or callipers or even a wheelchair – perhaps, perversely, things would have turned out better for me. Sure, there would still have been bullies, but there would also have been kindness and compassion. It takes a very extreme sort of bully to stoop to torment someone in a wheelchair. But those who were just a *bit* strange, a *bit* odd, a *bit* weird and clumsy – we were absolutely fair game for all but the very kindest and meekest children.

I'm not going to jump on the 'disabled' bandwagon. That's not what this is about. Please don't feel sorry for the poor disabled child. Don't talk about how terrible it was to bully a child with cerebral palsy. The cerebral palsy is *irrelevant* here. If it's more shocking that I had a mild disability, that would mean it would be slightly *less* shocking if I hadn't. And that is unacceptable. Bullying is bullying, whether you are disabled, able-bodied, black, white, gay, straight or whatever.

So, be outraged that I was bullied, but please don't be extra outraged that I was *disabled* and bullied. That would imply that those poor bullied 'normal' children deserve less sympathy, and I'm sure bullying hurts just as bad when it doesn't have a special label.

CHAPTER 3

I don't remember how it all started. I'm sure as a very young child at primary school I had plenty of friends and life was like that of any other normal little girl. I remember birthday parties and girls coming round for tea, and my going to theirs. But at some point, I do know that children in primary school started turning against me.

I don't know exactly when it started. But I know who started it. Vicky Simpson – the bane and nemesis of my life. Vicky was a year older than me, yet in primary school she had been kept down to repeat a year. I was never quite sure why this was. She was not the most academic of children, but neither was she bottom of the class. Her younger brother was also in my class, and they were always together. She was protective of him, in a slightly tough-girl way. Because she was a year older, she was the absolute leader, the toughest, most dominating, the queen of the entire year. Everyone looked up to her, everyone did as she said, and everyone was at least slightly afraid of her.

I had never been a hugely popular child. There had already been the odd comment about my slightly peculiar movements and a few 'why do you talk funny?' questions, but until this point, I was well tolerated by most of the children. Little children are usually very tolerant of differences of all kinds.

It was after a birthday party of mine, perhaps my ninth or tenth, to which the whole class had been invited – Vicky included – that I think it all really kicked off. The party was much like any other little girl's party with games and a large, unhealthy feast put out on paper plates. Meat paste sandwiches, pineapple and cheese on sticks, mini sausages, chocolate fingers, crisps, and big jugs of Ribena. But the birthday cake was a little different from most. My mother had a habit of making proper home-made cakes in shapes like cars, forts, trains and animals rather than buying in shop-made cakes like most other mothers. I was both grateful and annoyed with her for the cakes she always made us. It was lovely that she went to the care and trouble of making a proper cake. But if I'm honest, all I wanted was a cardboard-tasting pink fondant covered sponge from the supermarket. I think this time she had made a chocolate icing covered hedgehog-shaped cake, with little almond flakes sticking out all over it to look like prickles. Mum had put a lot of work into planning and making it. But to be fair, this cake really was a bit young for me at that age.

It was after this perfectly normal little girl's birthday party that Vicky changed towards me, irrevocably.

'Your cake was *stupid,*' she said at school afterwards. 'Why didn't your mum buy a proper cake? Can't she afford it?'

I said nothing, burning with embarrassment. But Vicky went on, 'And when you were dancing you looked like such a spastic. You *are* a spastic.'

There were quite a few laughs from the other children.

'Ha ha: *spastic!*'

And that was that. The class turned gradually against me and my fate was set. It was as if my mild oddities, which had never even been noticed before, had suddenly become painfully apparent. From that day forward, I became the butt of jokes, the one left out of games, the one who spent break times alone. My bag was thrown in the mud. My paintings taken home to show my parents were ripped up. My crisps were stolen at break time. I heard the term 'spastic' used almost every day. I think many of these primary age children didn't even know what 'spastic' meant. But they still thought it sounded funny and clever to call me that. And whatever Vicky said, the other children would repeat like little parrots.

What's really odd is that Vicky Simpson, like most bullies, was not especially clever, or pretty. She was over-tall and big, like me. But she also had bulbous eyes and a huge mouth that made her look a bit like a frog. Her hair was mousy like mine, but cut short, like a boy's. She certainly wasn't academically talented, and was toward the bottom of the class in reading and maths. I remember she was good at drawing cartoons, and she did have a knack for making people laugh. But other than that, she wasn't exceptional in any way. In another world, another town, another slightly different set of circumstances, *she* could easily have been the bullied one. And perhaps that was it; perhaps she bullied me because she knew she was only one step away from being bullied herself.

What I'll never understand is why so many of the others went along with her. Why did children suddenly turn against me simply because Vicky took a dislike to me? I wish I knew. I'd like to say it was just the weak and easily led children at primary school that copied Vicky Simpson's bullying. But that's not really true. Once it had started, everyone else, almost the entire year, naturally joined in, as if it was perfectly 'right'. It was almost as if all along they had been resisting the temptation, but now that my faults had been publicly acknowledged and picking on me was 'allowed', they weren't going to hold back any longer.

CHAPTER 4

PE lessons were a particularly bad memory for me. Because of my awkward movements, many of the sports were very difficult. I could run and jump okay. I could also skip very fast and accurately when the dinner ladies would turn a rope for us at lunchtime, singing skipping songs. But because of the mild disability, my hand-eye coordination was almost non-existent, and anything that involved throwing was particularly difficult. Of all childhood activities, this particular action – *throwing* – was almost impossible for me. I would take the ball and make the throwing movement, just like I had seen other children do. But despite my best efforts, the ball would inevitably fly off in a weird direction, or even up in the air. Whether I was throwing a small rounders ball or a big football, I just couldn't get the damn thing to travel in the direction I wanted. Sometimes I even dropped the ball behind me over the back of my shoulder while trying to throw to someone. During PE and Games lessons, this would elicit either whoops of laughter and amusement, or stamping and exclamations of anger from the other children, depending which team they were on.

Worst of all of my torments at primary school was swimming lessons. Our school had its own modest 25-metre swimming pool, open air, and surrounded by a breezeblock wall. The pool was heated but our school was situated in a fairly lonely spot on the top of a hill, and the wind whistled and screamed around that little pool. I don't seem to remember ever swimming in the sunshine; I only remember shivering my way to the pool in the freezing winter. Whichever teacher was taking the swimming class would often be bundled up in a thick anorak and scarf, stamping his or her feet as they watched us splash about, 'learning to swim'.

I don't think swimming lessons were fun for anyone, especially in the cold weather, but they were doubly traumatic for me. I was not only cursed with a mild disability, I was also cursed with early puberty. At the age of seven my mother took me to the doctor to discuss my overly developed breasts. (He said there was nothing wrong and sent us away.) The first pubic hairs arrived by nine and my periods started at ten. Taking me to the doctor to discuss such things did nothing to help my feelings of normality. I seriously thought there was something terribly wrong with me. I certainly thought I was the only girl in the world to have pubic hair at the age of nine.

Changing for swimming was a terrible ordeal for those of us with early puberty. Because swimming lessons meant *getting naked*. The changing rooms for swimming were in a separate building from the school, up on the side of the hill next to the pool itself. The building was an unheated concrete block, freezing and unfriendly. The design of the interior of this changing room block would be unthinkable today. It was made up of two concrete rooms, one for the girls, one for the boys. But the two rooms were adjoining with a short, wide corridor connecting them. There were no doors at the ends of the corridor, which meant the interior of the block was completely open-plan.

So not only could any boy take a sneaky look up the corridor to watch the girls changing, but one or other of them would often run into the girls' area to take a quick closer look. They would end up in trouble for this, but they were never seriously punished; anyway, it never seemed to stop them. I lived in terror of boys coming into the room and seeing me naked. Dealing with the girls was hard enough, but allowing a boy to see my body was unthinkable. It's not that I was afraid of nakedness itself; it was what was attached to my naked body that I couldn't bear them to see – my breasts and my horrible, horrible pubic hair.

Of course, part of my shyness was down to the mortification at having been taken to the doctor as a child to discuss my freakishly different bodily changes. But I can't blame all of my shyness on my mother. I blame it on an instance in primary school where the other children first got to learn of the state of my body.

I had been changing under a towel when Vicky Simpson snatched it away from me, leaving me standing there naked. 'Oh my god, *look!*' screamed Vicky. 'Look at her horrible pubes!' The other girls crowded round me, screeching with laughter and feigned over-exaggerated disgust.

'Ugh, you look revolting with that hairy fanny,' Vicky went on. 'What's wrong with you? You make me want to throw up.' Vicky then made a puking noise, like she was pretending to be sick at the sight of my body.

Funnily enough, not all girls with early puberty suffered in the same way. I do remember one girl, Trudy Locke, looking over and saying, 'Hmph! Mine's hairier than *that!*' But one was interested in Trudy's body. It wasn't funny to mock her. It was only funny to mock me, the odd one, the weird one, the spastic. For me, pubic hair was a source of humiliation and ridicule. For Trudy, it was a source of pride. I always thought it was so unfair the way that works.

Usually, I would cope with impending swimming lessons by ensuring that I wore a skirt to school. That made changing easier, because it was nothing to take your knickers off underneath your skirt, and then pull up your swimming costume. That's what most girls did and no one looked twice at that. The horrible mistake came on those days that I forgot I had swimming and Mum made me wear trousers or jeans to school. That meant having to wrap a towel around myself as I pulled down my pants. Or it meant standing naked in front of the other girls, my shameful pubic hair on show to all. So often Vicky would pull the towel away as I stood there, and then scream with disgust at my perfectly normal body.

Other girls just stripped off, without a thought or a care, standing with their straight, little white hairless bodies, talking to each other. I so wanted to be like them, flat and boyish, not womanly like I was – overly tall, a bit chubby, with breasts and hair everywhere. I felt I was an ugly lump, a huge chunk of disgusting flesh. Freakish, unclean, unfeminine. Thanks to Vicky Simpson I hated my perfectly normal body for almost my entire childhood, and even into adulthood.

CHAPTER 5

I almost never cried at primary school. Even when the bullying was particularly spiteful, and my heart was breaking with misery, I always fought to keep the tears back. Not crying when bullied, hurt, or told off by a teacher was a matter of great pride – a very serious matter.

Crying would only have made things much, much worse, or so I thought. Those who cried over such things were deemed 'crybabies' and even tormented for their emotional outbursts. I remember Vicky's gang turning on one little girl, Lorraine, who had cried when she fell over and scuffed her knees. In unison, they all bent their knees, dropped to crouch on the floor around

Lorraine, sticking their thumbs in their mouths and crying out, 'Wah! Wah! Wah!' mimicking baby noises.

No, crying at being bullied was out of the question. It needed to be kept quiet, and any pain or misery had to be internalised and kept secret. Of course, this security was false. By not voicing my pain, it only meant that teachers rarely noticed what was going on and most of Vicky's behaviour to me went unnoticed.

Throughout my final year of primary school, Vicky tormented me constantly. She and her ever-present little gang would sometimes spend an entire lunchtime crowded around me, trapping me in the corner of two walls by the water fountain. Vicky often stood guarding this water fountain, as if she owned the rights to it. If any child came up to get some water, she would only allow them to drink once they had asked her nicely. Sometimes she refused and sent them away without drinking.

At this point, the attacks on me were mainly verbal.

'Hey, *Shitvorn.*'

'Why are you such an ugly *freak?*'

'You're such a spastic!'

'Everyone hates you!'

'One day, we're going to get you.'

'My brother's going to get his mates to kill you.'

Even when I managed to spend a lunchtime playing with other children, Vicky's gang would often be standing nearby, arms folded across their chests, scowling at me with pursed lips and hate in their eyes.

In all the time that I knew her as a child, I don't think I ever saw Vicky alone. Through a combination of charm, humour, manipulative flattery and menacing, she always managed to recruit a loyal band of followers who trailed her wherever she went and obeyed every order she gave. At the age of ten and eleven, Vicky's power over others was really quite extraordinary. Even the teachers seemed to be impressed by Vicky. She would answer them back, mess around in class, and really be very cheeky in front of them. Somehow, most of the time she got away with it. Behaviour that would never have been tolerated from other children was somehow totally acceptable from Vicky.

Occasionally, Vicky's behaviour or bullying did get noticed by the teachers and she would be instructed to leave me alone, or they would tell her to stand by the wall. This primary school punishment entailed standing, for an indeterminate period of time, with your face to the wall in full view of the rest of the class. For most children, standing against the wall was a thing of great shame – a very bad punishment for such young children. But even as she stood facing the wall, supposedly 'thinking about what she had done', Vicky always seemed to have a way of turning on the charm and making everyone laugh. She would put on a funny voice or dance in a silly way as she stood there, wiggling her bum or wrapping her arms around herself pretending to be kissing someone. When the other children laughed, she would then turn and smirk at the teacher who would say in an exasperated way, 'Oh, come on then, Vicky, back to your table. No point in standing there if you aren't going to be quiet.' Any bullying incident would soon be forgotten as Vicky turned back to entertaining the class.

As a little child, it didn't cross my mind that I was being 'bullied'. I think I just assumed there truly was something really horribly wrong with me that made people not like me. I tried hard to be like the other children, to look like them, to dress like them and talk like them. I copied the ones I admired. I so wanted to be normal, to be just like everyone else. Instead I felt different, odd, strange, like a different species of child altogether. No wonder no one liked me, I imagined – I was far too different. And it was all my fault, or so I thought at the age of ten.

I lived for the weekends and home, where I was normal and felt accepted. I rarely met other children out of school. I just stayed at home with my lovely, lovely mum and helped her make cakes and cook the dinner. My mum was so sweet and gentle and she had a lovely singing voice. She could also play the piano and sometimes she would sing and play for us all.

My dad worked long hours and sometimes he had left for work before I got up and came home after I went to bed. Most of the time I only really saw him at the weekends. He was a serious, quiet man but he was always really happy when Mum sang and played piano for us. He also loved to play Scrabble and Chess. I often played with him even though I didn't really enjoy these games. It meant I got to spend some time with him and to see him smile.

When Mum and Dad weren't entertaining us, I would generally just watch an awful lot of television. Or I would sit in the bedroom I shared with my sister and listen to tapes or draw pictures. I played a lot with my older sister, Michaela, and my little brother, Sean. My sister was quite a bit older than me, aged 15 at that time. She was usually kind to me. And I absolutely loved my little brother, who was very cute and funny. We three sometimes put on plays together and created songs to perform to our parents. I sometimes liked to dress Sean up in dresses for these performances, and even sometimes put make-up on him. Dad said I would 'turn him fruity', but Mum always laughed at how cute he looked. And Sean never seemed to mind.

It was strange how idyllic things were at home while school was so, so different. Home and school were like different worlds. It was such a happy house. Everyone loved me and I loved them. I entertained people and they entertained me. I laughed a lot and made people laugh in return. At home no one called me freak or spastic. No one thought I was different. I was just Siobhan. Home was the only place I was truly happy.

CHAPTER 6

It was a miserable last year at school. But eventually, the end of the fourth year came (what is these days called year six). It meant we were moving on, to new schools, to *big school*. Most of the class was moving to the big next-door comprehensive, literally across the road from our primary. But something wonderful was about to happen in my world. My parents had decided we needed four bedrooms so we three children could each have our own room. My family were moving house, and in the summer holiday we would be moving to a new village. We had been to see the new house already. It was only a smallish new-build, with very tiny bedrooms. But it seemed enormous to me at the time, almost like a palace. I was so proud to be moving there. But the best thing of all, the most *wonderful* thing of all was that this village was in a different catchment area. I would be going on to a different school from the entire rest of the class.

I could start all over again.

There would be no Vicky Simpson.

No one would know who I was.

I could be anyone I wanted.

I even had a wonderful plan I intended to carry out in preparation for my new life. I would change my name. I had hated my name for as long as I can remember: *Siobhan.* Of course, these sorts of Irish names are common now. Thanks to Sinead O'Connor and Niamh Cusack, no one thinks twice about someone being a *Sinead* or a *Niamh* or indeed, a *Siobhan.* But back in the late '70s and early '80s, everyone was utterly bemused by my name.

I remember one particularly ignorant teacher, Mr Jacks, needing to call out my name in a school assembly. I, along with about a dozen others, had passed my cycling proficiency test and Mr Jacks was handing out the badges and certificates. Children were getting up as their names were called out, and walking to the front to collect their awards. Each child received a hearty round of applause. As my turn came round, you could see Mr Jacks' irritation as he attempted to pronounce my name.

'Sy - oh - ban? See - oh - ban? Oh…I can't say this!' he finally gave up in frustration. 'Can't you just use a normal name at school?'

And to Vicky, I had always been *Shitvorn.*

So I had this fantasy that on arriving at my new school, I would tell the others I was called something else. The form teacher would read out my name *Siobhan Louise Lennon.* And he or she would ask, 'Is it Siobhan or Louise?'

All I needed to do was say *Louise* and I could leave that horrible name behind. I could start a new life as Louise, and be normal, like all the Emmas and the Joannes and the Katies.

I remember that very first day at my new secondary school. I was sitting in the form room, just another face amongst many. No one knew me yet. The teacher, Miss Russell, was taking the register. As it was the very first time the register was being taken, she was calling out our names in full, and then asking which particular name we were to be known by. The Katherines got to be Kathy, Katie or Kate. Thomas became Tom. Of the two Jameses one asked to be called Jamie. And some children used their middle names.

All I had to do was tell them I was known as Louise. I never stopped to think how unworkable it would be having a different name at school to home. I hadn't discussed it with anyone. I hadn't really thought it through. But it felt like a wonderful fantasy to me, and I was excited about my big plan for starting my new life as a different person.

As my turn to answer loomed, my heart began to pound. And as Miss Russell started to read out my name, I was determined to carry on with the plan.

I sat waiting for the teacher to look at my name, do a double take and think for a moment before answering. I had seen it so many times before. I could almost see the thought process going on in a person's mind. *How do I pronounce this?*

But rather than stumbling or hesitating, Miss Russell read out my first name, *Siobhan,* beautifully, just as naturally as if it were a name she said every day. I was so surprised to hear a stranger get my name right first time that my plan became forgotten. 'That's right,' I blurted out. And then, embarrassed, added 'I'm called Siobhan.'

So much for my plan to change my name.

But as it turned out, the whole 'weird name' thing wasn't so much an issue at this school. In my class I had an Imelda and a Rayanne – both much more outlandish names than mine, I thought. Once they had got used to it, no one batted an eye at *Siobhan*.

My new school was rougher than the previous one. Most of the girls were from the big council estate and there was quite a bit of fighting and bad behaviour. There was a lot of swearing and spitting, even by the girls. Some of the children smoked upstairs on the school bus and disappeared off behind the gym building at lunchtime to puff on cigarettes. But I didn't mind about any of that. Because in this school I was experiencing something completely new: total acceptance. I had friends, a whole group of them. I never ate lunch alone, I walked home with a group of girls, I was invited around after school on Friday afternoons and I invited girls back. I was even getting by in sport when it was discovered that despite my awkwardness, I was a half decent middle distance runner. Tennis and netball were still an embarrassing ordeal but my athletics ability gave me just enough credibility to avoid ever being ridiculed. At the end-of-year sports day, I won the 1500-metre race and very briefly became something of a superstar. I had a place. I was one of them. I was just like everyone else, not considered ugly or freakish. My primary school bullying was behind me and I felt almost normal, for the first time in my life.

It wasn't that this was a kinder school than my previous primary, far from it. Bullying still happened every day. But the children in this school just didn't bully *me.* In this school, it seemed, it was overweight kids who bore the brunt of the bullying. Fat kids and posh kids.

There was an overweight, clever posh boy called Richard Harris who spent all his break times reading crime novels, locked in a cubicle, sitting on the toilet. Richard was absolutely terrified of spiders, and having discovered this phobia by accident the other bullies went out of their way to collect every spider they could find out on the grass and in the dusty corners, to throw down at him as he sat reading. He would scream like a little girl and then cry. I often think about poor Richard now.

I wonder if he has done something wonderful with his clever brain. I do hope so.

There was a properly deranged boy, David Pascoe, two years up from me. He had a half-crazed look in his eye, walked everywhere at a thousand miles an hour and sometimes spoke to the walls. He was tormented mercilessly, chased, his property stolen, his head held down the toilet while others pulled the flush. It later turned out he was properly mentally ill. I won't reveal his eventual future crime for fear of identifying him, but David is now in Broadmoor prison for the criminally insane.

So as you can see, amongst all these other social rejects, I just wasn't interesting enough to single out for bullying. Why pick on a tall, slightly gauche girl when there were properly crazy kids and fat posh arachnophobes to pick on?

I do regret now that I didn't stand up for these bullied children. I hated to watch as they were tortured daily. I am ashamed to say I didn't lift a finger or say a word to stop the torment of David or Richard or any of the others. I just stood by while it happened.

Why didn't I stand up for them?

If you don't know the answer to that then you probably don't remember just how precarious is the balance between total social acceptance and total social rejection at secondary school. I'm sorry, Richard. I'm sorry, David. But I just couldn't risk upsetting that delicate balance and losing my newfound status as a normal, everyday pupil. I was just so relieved not to be on the receiving end this time.

As I've said before, I was not the most popular child in the school. I wasn't in the coolest social groups or one of the 'leaders'. But in that first year, not one person singled me out for bullying. I was a bit of a no one. I had quite a few friends and no one hated me. That was more than enough, and that first year at secondary was the happiest of my entire school life.

CHAPTER 7

It was in the second year (what is now called year 8) of my new school that everything changed. Something happened that set my life on a new nightmarish course that would last for three whole years.

It was the first day of that second year at school and the class was all abuzz with activity. There were twittering voices, there was laughter and lots of general excitement at seeing each other again after the long summer holiday. Our new form teacher came in to introduce himself and take the register. His name was Mr Batts. He had a big bushy beard, was quite short and round, and he seemed like a bit of a softy. A bit of a Father

Christmas character. I took an instant liking to him, although that affection would be short-lived.

Mr Batts told us we were also having two new pupils in the class this term. A boy and a girl. As the new girl was brought in, we all craned our necks to look at the new oddity, the new addition. What did she look like? Was she pretty or frumpy? Was she short or tall? Was she going to be *our* friend? I'm sure we were all thinking the same thing.

My heart leapt until I felt it was physically sitting in the back of my throat. I was almost sick.

The new pupil was Vicky Simpson.

She had a sort of self-satisfied swagger as she came in. A smirk on her face. Less like a shy newcomer and more like a potential new gang leader. On seeing me, her face lit up with recognition

'Right, *Shitvorn?*'

A couple of the other children tittered in amusement.

'Ah, you two already know each other, good,' said the dopey Mr Batts, ignoring the insult. 'Siobhan, let Vicky sit next to you. You can look after her.'

If there was one person on earth who didn't need looking after it was Vicky Simpson. By the end of the day she had removed herself from the shame of sitting next to me and found herself a more suitable companion to sit with. By the end of the week, she had a new posse of best friends, a gaggle of girls hugely impressed with her confidence and charisma and proud to be associated with her. By the end of a month or two, she was running the place.

She and her younger brother had been moved out of their previous school due to 'an incident' that even Vicky wouldn't talk about. She just proudly told us, 'The other school couldn't handle me. So I had to come here.' I never found out what really happened at her previous school.

She fast became one of the 'leaders' of the school, one of those powerful, dominant kids that everyone looked up to. The ones who you wanted to be your friend, the ones who could command other kids to do their bidding, and always got their own way. I refuse to call them 'alpha' as in 'alpha male' and 'alpha female' because that almost seems to venerate them. The truth was that while some of these leader kids were clever, funny, charismatic and great to be around, others were merely spiteful bullies, perhaps even fledgling criminals. So while some leader kids inspired respect, others just inspired fear. Vicky was the most dangerous of all; she was both funny and charismatic and as mean and manipulative as a little serial killer: a thirteen-year-old psychopath.

The role of a leader kid would be fascinating to an anthropologist or someone wanting to study basic human society. The power of a kid like Vicky Simpson meant that she got to dictate who got bullied and who didn't. If she decided to take a liking to crazy David Pascoe, everyone else would like him too. If she decided to take a dislike to the previously unnoticed, tall mousy girl with the funny Irish name and the slightly strange walking gait, everyone else would dislike her too.

And that's exactly what happened. We were in the class on a rainy lunch break, sitting on the desks as we always did, in our little groups, chatting and messing about.

'Hey, Shitvorn,' Vicky's voice struck horror into me. 'You still got that massive hairy fanny?' And then, turning to the rest of the class, said, 'You seen her fanny? She was like a fucking gorilla in primary. It's most probably down to her knees by now!'

The class laughed, like kids always do at crude, rude jokes. And from then on, things just escalated. Once again, just as had happened at primary school, the class started to turn against me.

It was happening all over again.

I still had a few friends, but some of my weaker minded chums started to move away from me, probably for fear of being bullied themselves. Others who had never been particularly friendly to me completely went along with Vicky and even joined in with the bullying. Eventually it got to the stage where the majority of the class were picking on me, if not out-and-out bullying. Most now called me *Shitvorn,* and I had become the butt of class jokes. *What's the difference between Siobhan Lennon and a bucket of shit? Haha! Nothing!*

Games and PE loomed in the week every Wednesday afternoon. Triple games. The absolute worst day of the week. Even though in the previous term I had proved myself as a fast and fit runner, I was now being chosen last in that hateful games lesson team-picking exercise. The simple act of making children pick teams, one at a time, has to be one of the cruellest acts possible. Who thought this up and in what universe was this *ever* acceptable behaviour? If you were once a games teacher and you made children do this, I hope you feel suitably ashamed. It really is a form of child abuse.

In my experience, games teachers often seemed to have a sadistic streak in them. At our school, the biggest girls were always made to carry the kit and equipment. We big awkward girls had to lug the smelly kit ahead of everyone else, like hulking great men, while the twittering little fairy girls got to prance and giggle their way over to the playing field, or the netball courts, complimenting each other on their new trainers.

My PE and Games performance deteriorated rapidly. The winter sports were worse, generally – anything that involved throwing was always a nightmare for me, and netball, with its rapid-fire movements, was impossibly difficult for a girl whose movements were necessarily slow and deliberate. I couldn't throw for toffee. Throwing things had always been a big problem but now I had become so nervous it became even worse. When a netball was thrown my way, I would panic, chucking it aimlessly away from me, to the other team or even straight up into the air. This inevitably invoked screams of laughter or angry disappointed insults as I lost possession of the ball for my team.

'Fucking hell, Shitvorn!'

'Are you a spastic or something.'

'Don't pass it to her, she'll just fuck it up.'

It really was starting all over again. All of it.

Just like primary school. I was the odd one, the clumsy one, the spastic, the freak.

I honestly believe none of this would ever have happened had it not been for Vicky Simpson joining our school. Not everyone joined in. In fact, a lot of the other girls kept away from Vicky. Even Vicky's own brother never bullied me although he had often seen her do it. They were close as siblings, and she clearly adored him, but he was not ruled by her like the other children were. He was never part of her gang. In fact, I remember that Vicky's brother sometimes made a point of leaving the room when she staged an attack.

But such was her power that Vicky managed to maintain a constant posse of cronies surrounding her. When one left her clutches, as they sometimes did, she always managed to recruit another within days. I would see it happen. Vicky would approach someone new, often a weak, friendless girl – someone a bit lost, a bit left out – and she would befriend them. Using flattery and persistence, she would quickly win them over. She would make them feel privileged and special to be singled out by someone so popular. And within days, the unpopular and lonely new girl would have a whole group of friends and an apparently strong and popular best friend in Vicky Simpson. No wonder they couldn't resist. Looking back it was fascinating really; Vicky was a real little Machiavelli.

And then, the new recruit would turn on me. It was almost like one of those films about prison or street gangs. The latest of Vicky's gang would then commit an act of bullying toward me, or to one of the other bullied kids. Looking back, I have often wondered if these were a sort of initiation ritual.

Every day it would happen. Sometimes I would be accosted before school, sometimes after, sometimes during breaks. Sometimes it was all of these. I would go through each day just waiting for the next attack. Sometimes it was physical – a subtle punch in the back as we were queuing to enter a class. Often it was mental – finding a note taped to the inside of my desk lid: *'Shitvorn Lennon is an ugly spastic'.* There were the constant verbal digs, dozens every day.

'Hey, freak, are they all spastics in your family?'

'Can you actually do spells, like curses and stuff?'

'Why don't you just kill yourself, freak?'

'Can't you go to a special school for flids and leave us all alone?'

'God, what's that stink? Is that Siobhan's breath?'

'No, it's her fanny! Ha ha ha!'

And then there was the weird stuff.

I'd find a bloodied tampon in my pencil case.

Dog shit inside my desk.

And sometimes I'd put my hand to the back of my head and find a huge gob of phlegm and spit on the back on my hair. I once arrived home to find such a mess on the back of my school jumper. I had walked all the way home from school with it dribbling down my back.

CHAPTER 8

Why didn't I just tell someone? Sometimes people really don't get it. It seems so straightforward when you're an adult – all you need to do is tell someone, didn't you know?

If you're bullied at school, just tell a teacher, tell your parents or tell a 'responsible adult'. Then something will be done, all your problems will go away and everyone will be best friends forever. Right?

Wrong.

First I told a teacher. I told one of my favourite teachers, the French mistress, Miss Bosch. She was a very kindly lady and listened intently and seriously to my story. I told her the lot, from primary school to the present day. I told her everything: about all the attacks, the verbal abuse, the disgusting things put in my desk, and all my worries about what would happen next. I told her that sometimes I thought about playing truant or running away just so that I didn't have to come to school.

And having listened carefully and thoughtfully, Miss Bosch proceeded to spout the usual dogma, all that clichéd crap about the best way of dealing with bullies.

'You just need to learn to stand up for yourself, Siobhan,' she said. 'Don't let it get to you. Just be more confident and don't let her bother you. Why don't you just ignore her and stay away from her?' And then she wisely added, 'You know, she probably only does it because she's jealous of you. She probably just wants to be your friend.'

Yeah, right. Thanks, Miss Bosch. What an excellent analysis of the situation: *she just wants to be your friend.* That advice was as helpful as a hole in the head.

Finally, I told my mum. Or rather, she found out. I came home one day sopping wet. I had walked, dripping, all the way home from school after Vicky's gang had dragged me to the swimming pool and pushed me in. They threw my school bag after me.

I couldn't think of a suitable lie so I had to tell Mum the truth. I told her everything. I told her about the way Vicky and her gang had been tormenting me since primary school. I'm not sure she believed me at first. But once she could see I was telling the truth, she started to cry. She was such a gentle woman. I remember feeling so bad for upsetting her and wished I hadn't said a word. It wasn't fair that she had to suffer too.

She called the school next morning to speak to the headmaster, Mr Pengelly. As a result, a meeting was called with me, Mum, Vicky, her mum and dad, and our form teacher, Mr Batts.

Our headmaster always thought he was rather cool. I think he had aspirations of becoming one of those amazing, inspirational heads who takes on a struggling school and turns it around. He rarely disciplined children in his office. He was far too cool and progressive for that. So we all sat in an area he had created called 'the lounge' that had soft armchairs rather than hard school chairs. All seven of us were crammed in there for the meeting.

Mr Pengelly kicked off the proceedings. 'What's this all about, Vicky?' he asked. 'Why did you push Siobhan into the pool? Don't you know that was dangerous to push someone in the pool fully clothed? She could have drowned.'

'It was only a joke, and I didn't mean it,' Vicky lied. 'We were playing around, daring each other. It was *Siobhan's* idea! We wanted to help her get dried but she just ran off.' And then she added with mock sincerity and a pained look on her face, 'I'm really sorry, Siobhan.'

What an actress she was.

'What about these other incidents?' the head went on, 'Siobhan says you put a condom in her desk.'

'But she put one in mine first,' lied Vicky indignantly. 'I was just getting her back!'

And on it went, every crime I had reported was brought up and Vicky would answer with a perfect excuse in the most reasonable, almost exasperated way, as if she couldn't understand why I was being so mean. Sometimes she just looked blankly, as if trying to recall something, and then said completely convincingly, 'No, I don't think that was me. I don't remember that at all. Siobhan, *I* didn't do that.'

God, she was good.

Before long, the head was satisfied he had heard enough. 'So, it looks like we have a case of six of one and half-a-dozen of the other, doesn't it, girls? Vicky, will you agree to go easy on Siobhan? And you, Siobhan, will you agree not to be so sensitive from now on? Not everyone's out to get you, you know.'

And then he uttered that stupid, moronic, pointless order that adults seem to think will solve all the problems of the classroom.

'Now, girls, shake on it.'

Shake on it? What is that supposed to do? It's something businessmen and salesmen and estate agents do when they want to sell you something.

To twelve and thirteen-year-old girls, it is completely meaningless.

Vicky immediately held out her hand to me. 'Come on, Siobhan, shake hands, make friends!' she said sweetly.

And that was it. The pompous headmaster had done his job. He could proudly put a tick in his book, that he, Steven Pengelly, this excellent headmaster, had dealt properly and effectively with an alleged case of bullying and managed to get the two silly little girls to shake hands, all within forty-five minutes. What a wonderful, clever man he was.

What a moron. What a ridiculous, pointless man.

Because the truth was, everything got so much worse from then on. Now Vicky only bullied me when we were completely alone and no adults or teachers were around. But when teachers were even remotely in earshot, she would feign friendship toward me.

'Who wants to come to the shopping precinct on Saturday? We're going to buy shoes. Siobhan, do you want to come with us?'

'Come on, Siobhan, sit next to me,' she'd offer as Mr Batts walked into the room, five minutes after she'd been holding my face down on the desk by my hair.

'Come on, Siobhan, you can see Vicky's trying to be your friend,' Mr Batts would say. 'You've got to do your bit too, you know.'

So I would sit down, next to a smiling Vicky. And she would instantly show me a note she had written. *Playground. Break time. You're dead, bitch.* Then she would scrunch up the note and put the paper in her bag and smile back at Mr Batts.

Vicky never made empty threats. If she said she would get me at break time, she would get me at break time. Moments after the bell rang she would be looking for me, usually with Sam, Emma and Sharon, sometimes with many more. For a long time, I remember always trying to find somewhere new to hide from her on the school grounds. But eventually I gave up hiding just so that I could get the attack over with. Sometimes I was held down while rubbish, apples cores and crisp bags were rained down onto me from one of the bins. Sometimes I was physically punched or kicked. But usually, I was just held against the wall of the gym, down the alleyway by the tennis courts where dinner ladies and teachers rarely ventured, and verbally abused with the nastiest things they could think of.

'You're so ugly, you make me want to be sick.'

'Sharon saw your dad bumming a man in the park. He's a queer, your dad.'

'Why don't you kill yourself, and do us all a favour?'

'Why didn't your mum have an abortion, freak? Didn't she know she was having a spastic baby?'

Then they would all push me tight against the wall and order me to say something, like *I'm a spastic.* Or *I'm a lesbian.* Or *I eat shit sandwiches.* Or they would just make me squeak like a pig and wouldn't let me go until I did.

The thing was, Vicky almost never bullied me *all* break time or *all* lunchtime. Sometimes at lunch break a bullying session might last quarter of an hour. But usually, it was a short, intense attack lasting a few minutes. I think these short, vicious attacks acted to get the vindictiveness out of their systems, like a release, because, after this initial little spat of abuse, they would generally let me go and lose interest. Perhaps they then moved on to another child, perhaps they just got on with the day; I don't know. But I did know they probably wouldn't bother me again that break time. I'd breathe a small sigh of relief, safe in the knowledge that, for at least the next half hour or so, I was safe.

So, a fat lot of good telling my parents and teachers had been. I had turned the teachers slightly against me and only succeeded in making Vicky look like the magnanimous hero of the story. Vicky was the great peacemaker; she was the true friend to this odd, over-sensitive little girl. And worst of all, I had upset my dear sweet mother. I had made her cry, and that broke my heart.

CHAPTER 9

I didn't tell my mum about the dead seagull I found in my PE bag. I didn't tell her about the time my head was flushed in a dirty toilet bowel full of urine and toilet paper. I didn't tell her about all the days I went hungry because Vicky's gang had taken my packed lunch, stolen the chocolate biscuits and the crisps, and thrown the sandwiches in the bin. And I didn't tell her about the school trip.

Our music teacher, Mr Vogle, had arranged a trip to the ballet at a theatre in a town twenty miles away. I think he had aspirations of refining our tastes and turning us into cultured, sophisticated adults. He looked and dressed like an eighteenth-century composer with big foppish hair, and always had a handkerchief in his top pocket. Sadly for Mr Vogle, almost no one in our class had much time for music and his lessons were generally chaotic – just excuses to bash the hell out of his already battered glockenspiels and fling the beaters around the room.

Attendance on this trip wasn't compulsory but the whole class signed up to go to the ballet. I'm sure he was delighted that his class were finally showing such an interest in classical music. The truth was, we would have gone on a trip to watch paint dry if it meant getting out of school for the afternoon. Plus, the ballet was taking place on Wednesday afternoon. And that meant missing triple games. This was a dream come true for me and I was really looking forward to the prospect of a Wednesday without humiliation. I can't even remember what the ballet was called or which composer it was by. But that didn't matter – I was looking forward to the trip. We were to get on a coach straight after eating lunch and be driven to the theatre in time for the matinee performance. We were to get straight back on the coach afterwards and our parents were to pick us up from school at 5pm.

But it didn't go quite like that.

The day came. I had managed to eat my packed lunch at school without it being thieved by Vicky, and we went out in a line to the school gate to catch the waiting coach. As we boarded the coach, I immediately took a seat up towards the front of the coach so I could be near the two accompanying teachers, Mr Vogle and a lady supply teacher, who occupied the very front seats. I know this was where most of the 'swots' sat, the well-behaved, academic, unpopular children. But I didn't mind that. If I was up front, it meant I could sit in safety, being well away from Vicky and her gang, who of course sat along the back five seats of the coach.

The trip was like most school coach trips – excited, loud, and a little rambunctious. I was enjoying myself as much as anyone at this point. All went well until we got to the theatre. It was not a beautiful old Theatre Royal with red plush seats, tassels on the curtains and gold fittings; it was one of those ultra modern places with a huge atrium with a long, brightly lit bar and low, square coffee tables surrounded by modular seating covered in cheap orange fabric. We all gathered in the atrium around the two teachers, excitedly chatting. I could also see that we were not the only school party that had come for this performance. There appeared to be at least two other school groups, easily identifiable by their different coloured uniforms. The different school groups eyed each other suspiciously, as children of same age will often do.

I didn't even notice Vicky and her friends. I had other things on my mind and was blissfully unaware of what was about to happen. I didn't notice that she was walking ahead of me as we walked up the stairs, nor that she was still just slightly in front of me as we went through a narrow corridor on our way to the auditorium. I was walking towards the back of the group and most of the children and both of the teachers had already disappeared through the door to the auditorium. There were just a few of us still to enter.

I am not a hundred per cent sure what happened next. I heard Vicky's voice saying softly, *'Now!'* and Sam and Sharon moved out of the way, to the side of the corridor. Then something came swinging toward me. The next thing I knew I was being hit violently across my bare shins by something hard and metallic. There was a horrible thud as both my legs took the force of being hit by something heavy. I gasped and crumpled to the floor. I felt like my legs were broken. Vicky and almost all the others disappeared into the auditorium and the door shut. And then I saw the object she had hit me with. A fire extinguisher – a big, heavy, red fire extinguisher. There was blood running down one of my shins and both had visible dents from where the extinguisher had hit me.

Two girls, Toni Harris and Michelle Baker, stopped to help me, one of them disappearing and coming back with wet paper towels – the ubiquitous and totally ineffectual school remedy for injuries of all kinds. I was on the floor, crying with pain. But the performance was about to start and Michelle and Toni, both meek and quiet children, eventually left me on the floor. There was no teacher to be seen. The door of the auditorium closed again and I was left sitting alone in the corridor, crying and bleeding, in indescribable pain.

A few moments later, the same door opened and an usherette came out. She looked at me as if I were a piece of chewing gum on the carpet.

'What's the matter with you?' she said without a hint of sympathy. 'It's starting. You're going to miss it.'

'I… I hurt myself,' I sobbed.

'If you go down to the box office, they've got a first aid kit,' she said, walking away. That was the extent of her help.

I eventually dragged myself into the nearby toilets. I soon realised my legs weren't broken; they just were badly bruised and one of them had a nasty cut. I missed the entire first act of the ballet, just sitting on the toilet, weeping softly and holding wet paper towels to my shins.

Toni and Michelle came to find me in the interval and found me still in the loo. They had brought me a can of Coke.

'She's such a cow,' said Michelle, kindly. 'We didn't tell Sir. We thought you wouldn't want us to. She'd only go mad if we did.' I had to agree. Telling teachers about the bullying had never worked in the past.

The bleeding had stopped and I did re-enter the show with them to watch the second act, but I hardly noticed the dancing. It was all I could do not to cry. I spent the whole act trying to remain composed and not think about the spiteful attack that had just happened. I could feel a throbbing, ringing pain in my legs that lasted for hours afterwards.

I went home from that horrible event in a sort of depression. On the coach ride home I couldn't even speak. I felt so hated and so hateful. Why did Vicky despise me *so* much? What had I ever done to her? Why couldn't she just leave me alone, stay away from me? Vicky had never been this violent before and I was truly shocked and genuinely frightened now. What would she do next? Would she try to kill me?

I remember sitting in my room later that night, crying, making deals with God. I wasn't sure if God existed, or whether I believed in him, but I was willing to take a chance. I prayed to God and Jesus with the best, most heartfelt and truthful prayer I had ever given. I promised that if Vicky would stop bullying me, or would stay away from me, I would pray to Jesus and read the Bible every single day. I remember quite clearly how committed I felt to this promise. It actually made me feel a little calmer and more hopeful and I was sure this prayer, this promise would make a difference of some sort.

I took a gold crucifix that my auntie got me from my jewellery box and put it round my neck, as a sign of my commitment. I felt sure that Jesus would notice that.

CHAPTER 10

The astounding thing was that the prayer worked, at least for a while. That's how I saw it at the time, anyway. I honestly believed for some time after this that Jesus had answered my prayer. Because the very next day I experienced a sort of little miracle.

I remember it was Thursday morning after the ballet incident and I was feeling sick at the thought of having to go to school. This day, of all days, I just couldn't face it. I felt I'd had enough. The atmosphere at home with my family was so calm and friendly and different from school. It was like another world. I just wanted to stay in my nice little pink room with the (now rather childish) Pierrot duvet cover and the pink walls. I didn't want to leave the safety of my home and my lovely mum. I still hadn't told her about the attack at the ballet and so far no one at home had noticed the nasty bruises on my legs.

'Siobhan, come on love, you're going to be late,' Mum said, coming into my room and finding me still in my nightie. I felt so ashamed of the thought that my family, teachers and everyone at school would see the marks and ask where they had come from. I imagined the embarrassment I would feel when Vicky asked, probably in front of the whole class, 'How did you do that, Siobhan?' I couldn't let that happen.

'Mum, I don't feel very well,' I lied.

'What's wrong? You look okay.' I had to think fast, what did I feel? Sick? Tummy ache? Headache?

'I feel really dizzy,' I finally said. I don't know where it came from. But it turned out it was the perfect thing to say.

'Oh dear,' said Mum, really concerned. 'I do hope you're not getting ill like Michaela.' My sister had suffered from epilepsy all her life and took medication for it. She rarely had an attack these days but prior to the medication she would often get really dizzy, and then eventually faint unconscious for a few minutes. She didn't have grand mal fits and shake and convulse on the floor. Contrary to popular understanding, lots of epileptics never have full seizures or fits, and Michaela was one of them.

'Yeah, I feel like I'm going to faint,' I lied further.

'Okay, well get dressed when you are ready and I'll get you to the doctor later.'

God. Was it really *that* easy? All I had to do was fake an illness? Had Jesus really answered my prayer and given me the perfect way to stay out of school?

'Acting ill' was very easy for me because I had all of my older sister's real symptoms to copy. I knew the way she looked when she fainted. I knew the wobble that came into her voice when an 'attack' was imminent. I knew the spaced out look that she often had in her eyes afterwards. I had had a lifetime of watching epileptic attacks.

And I also knew how to get around my incredibly soft-hearted mother. The combination of my superb mimicking skills and my child's ability to work on my mother's weaknesses meant I could play my kindly mother in any way I wanted.

I don't remember much about that first appointment with our family GP. I just remember him immediately saying, 'I'll refer her to see Doctor Hess. Keep a close eye on her until the appointment comes through.' Doctor Hess was Michaela's epilepsy specialist.

Secretly, I was thrilled. I had found a way to keep away from Vicky's bullying. I could stay in the warm, comfortable sanctuary of my family. I kept up that 'dizzy attack' for a whole week, just staying at home with Mum, watching *Pebble Mill* with her or sitting on my bed, listening to my tapes.

My mother was good with illness. She wasn't the sort of mother to look at a child with flu, say, 'You'll be okay' and bundle her off to school with an extra jumper. She was the type of mother who bought Lucozade and barley sugar, comics and fruit. She would make up a bed on the sofa and bring down pillows and duvets, tissues and Olbas Oil. And she made chicken noodle soup for ill people always: something her own American mother had taught her. It was almost fun having a cold or flu with a mother like that.

After about a week, I returned to school.

'Get them to call me if you feel dizzy again, love,' Mum had offered. And of course, with an offer as tempting as that, it wasn't going to be long before I took her up on it.

CHAPTER 11

I think I got through a couple of days before the first major bullying attack occurred. It wasn't actually Vicky who carried it out this time. It was big Sam, one of her meanest and most loyal assistants.

In our school the doors of the classrooms all had a sort of catch on the floor that acted as a doorstop. Once the door was fully opened, the catch on the floor would 'click' and lock the door in place, open against the wall of the classroom. Once locked in place, we then had to stand on the catch to release it. Only then could we close the door.

This meant that when the door was fully opened, there was a perfect, person-sized space, the shape of a triangular prism on its end, locked behind the door. This provided the perfect space for bullies to hold their victims captured. Once the door was fully opened with a click, anyone trapped against the wall could not possibly escape without the help of someone else to stand on the catch and release the door. Held in this prison, the victim could then be easily tormented with insults, spitting through the gap that was left, or by having the contents of the classroom bin emptied over the top of the door onto them. Honestly, what idiot ever designed schools with such doors? Not someone who knew kids, that's for sure.

It was Sam who decided it was time for me to spend some time in the 'door prison'. It was lunch hour and there were quite a few kids just sitting chatting in the class on this rainy day. Sam was a big, overweight girl: quite tomboyish and very strong. She scared me almost as much as Vicky. Though she was quieter and less vindictive, she was physically powerful and capable of a high level of violence that, until recently, hadn't been Vicky's style.

I had bumped into Sam as I came in through the door of the class. Offended at my mistake, she immediately grabbed me by the jumper and started to push me toward the door. She didn't say a single word, but I knew what was coming. If I became trapped, I might spend the entire lunch break behind that door. I also had an added fear because I have always been a bit claustrophobic. It was nothing serious, but was enough to make the experience of a 'behind the door' imprisonment very upsetting.

As she pushed me, I wobbled and stumbled backwards. And then, without even thinking, I fell to the floor and pretended to faint. I lay there, motionless like a lizard 'playing dead', leaving Sam standing over me, not knowing what to do next. I heard the sounds of scraping chairs and excited children getting up and coming over to see what was going on. I had my eyes closed but I knew that children were surrounding me, lying there on the classroom floor.

'Is she dead?'

'What did you do, Sam?'

'Nah, she's just fainted.'

'You sure she's not dead?'

'Dunno, someone call Sir.'

There were a couple of pokes from toes and someone gave me a little shake. But other than that, no one touched me until Mr Walshingham, one of the PE teachers, who was on lunch duty, was called into the room. Knowing first aid, he rearranged me into the 'recovery position'; I was as floppy as a dead rag doll, limp and almost lifeless. I remember lying there, feeling how *nice* this felt. It was peaceful, surrendering to nothingness. I didn't need to fight anyone or say anything. And it felt *safe.* The more limp I was, the less I felt threatened. While like this, the other kids wouldn't touch me. I was in another world, almost like I truly had fainted unconscious.

Mr Walshingham shouted to one of the boys to go to the staff room to fetch another teacher, and then ordered everyone to leave the room.

There was soon more commotion, more people coming into the room, adults this time. There was some whispering and lots of voices saying, 'Siobhan, can you hear me?' Eventually, I started to stir and opened my eyes a crack.

'Siobhan, sweetheart, we've called an ambulance. Just relax, you don't need to try and move.' It was Miss Barker, one of the kinder teachers. She taught Home Economics and was very motherly.

I closed my eyes again and went back into my other-worldly sanctuary. This was wonderful. I felt so special, so loved, so important. There was not a child in the room to torment me, only caring adults. I had learned something here.

Illness was my power. I could get attention, love and safety from bullying – all through faking illness.

I was taken to the local hospital in an ambulance. I was a bit disappointed that they didn't use their blue lights and sirens on the trip. But by now, I had 'regained consciousness'. To keep up appearances, I still acted woozy and said very few words to the ambulance man as he sat with me in the back of the vehicle.

I was taken to Casualty and a doctor looked me over. Mum turned up, looking frantically worried. There were lots of discussions and some physical examinations. Lots of pushing my tummy and tapping on my chest. Some looking down my throat and in my ears, and they also took some blood from my hand. They couldn't find any veins in my arm. Someone brought me a cup of tea and some biscuits.

I loved every minute of it. Even the needles.

Mum left late and I stayed in a children's ward overnight. I ate dinner with the other children and watched some TV before going to bed in the hard, white hospital bed.

I went home the next day but didn't go back to school. A further appointment had been made for me to have something called an EEG. I knew Michaela had had these before. It involved having electrodes attached to your head to measure your brain activity.

It was just unspoken and accepted that I would stay home until the EEG appointment came through and the results were in. So I didn't even work hard to stay home from school.

That time spent at home was like a dream. Like a lovely, long holiday. I loved these days with just my mum. She didn't work. Like many other mothers at the time, she was a full-time housewife, while my dad worked from early morning till late at night. I got to spend every day alone with her. She was an overprotective mother and almost never left me alone at home, even though I was twelve years old by now. Sometimes Mum would take me shopping with her or to one of her appointments, or we would go out to lunch.

I knew I was taking advantage of my mum's good nature. I knew I was betraying her trust. But I honestly think that part of her enjoyed it too. She really seemed to love having someone to care for again.

Mum was always trying to cuddle my younger brother, even though he was eight years old and didn't want to be cuddled. She would try and make him sit on her lap and he would just say, 'Oh, Mu-um!' and pull away from her. But now she had someone to cuddle up on the sofa with, and most of the time she had a smile on her face. It must have been lonely all day without anyone to talk to, and now she had me for company all day. I do know it was wrong to use her in this way, but I like to think it wasn't really so bad for her.

And besides all that, the simple truth was that I was in too deep now. I had set something in motion that seemed to have a life of its own. Doctors, specialists, appointments, tests – things were happening faster than I could plan. It was out of my control now, out of my hands.

I almost began to believe I really was ill after all.

CHAPTER 12

Back in the '80s, waiting lists for specialist appointments weren't what they are now. I don't know how long it was before I got my EEG appointment but it didn't seem like very long at all. Perhaps I was deemed to be an emergency case.

The EEG test took place at the same hospital to which I had been taken by the ambulance, but in a completely different building. I was called into a treatment room by a doctor and a nurse, leaving my mum sitting outside in the waiting area.

I remember being prepared for the EEG by the nurse. She put a rusty-coloured rubber hat on my head, like a sieve with very big holes. Then she rubbed salty gel into my scalp and attached wires to the hat with clips. I really wanted to see myself in a mirror with all the electrodes attached, but there was not one in the room.

All I was thinking at this time was that I *had* to make them believe I really was ill. I couldn't let them find out I had made it all up and be sent back to school. So when they started flashing strobe lights in my eyes and asking me to breath in deeply, I did whatever I could to act strange. I twitched and pretended to panic. I breathed too quickly to make my heart beat faster. I made little whimpering noises and shook my head, as if the flashing lights hurt me.

We got the results of the EEG in Dr Hess's office some days later. This was the first time I had met the epilepsy specialist. He spoke in a foreign accent; I think he was German because he said his Vs like Ws.

'The results are positive, indicating temporal lobe epilepsy,' said Dr Hess. 'We should start medication immediately.'

I wasn't actually surprised. I knew I could make them believe I was truly ill. When it came to adults, I could make them think anything. Mum nodded, with a resigned look, and then gave me a sad little smile, as if to say *I suspected as much.* Poor little Siobhan. She was born with mild spasticity. Now she has epilepsy to contend with. I really was a pitiful little girl, cursed with so much bad luck.

I often wonder whether the fact I had mild cerebral palsy influenced the doctor's diagnosis. After all, you might expect someone with cerebral palsy to have other problems too. I wonder if they all might not have been so quick to judge me as epileptic had I not been born the wrong way round.

Dr Hess gave me a prescription for Primadone, an anti-epilepsy drug. I took one there and then in the doctor's office before Mum and I went home.

But more miracles were to come! Because the Primadone made me violently sick! I felt almost immediately nauseated and flu-like after taking it and I couldn't eat a thing without vomiting. I didn't even have to fake illness to keep out of school because the drug made me genuinely ill.

I don't remember how much later it was when I found myself back in Dr Hess's office to discuss changing my medication. But I do know I hadn't been back to school since the fainting incident.

I was told by Dr Hess to stop taking the Primadone, and instead he prescribed Tegretol and

Epanutin. And then, to my complete astonishment, Dr Hess said something I don't think anyone was expecting.

'It's best if we admit Siobhan immediately. The nurse will take her up to the ward now. Can you bring in some clothes and things later, Mrs Lennon?'

What? I was to be admitted to *hospital?*

This was just too easy now. I had faked an entire disease so perfectly that I was now actually to be put in hospital, all as a result of my lies.

Of course, it didn't seem like lies. I felt I had no option. I felt I *had* to do it. This was a matter of survival, and perhaps that is why it came so naturally to me. After all, human beings are capable of amazing things when they genuinely feel in danger.

So that very afternoon, without even going home first to collect anything, I was admitted to the children's ward of the local hospital. Even though I had been enjoying my time away from school, I didn't feel upset at leaving my home or my mum. On the contrary, I was quite simply thrilled by this new development. I felt important and special. It felt like I was playing a part in some great drama, in a film or on TV. This was going to be an *adventure.*

CHAPTER 13

The children's ward looked like the typical hospital ward you would see in old films: a large, long rectangular room with rows and rows of beds on either side. There were probably twelve or fourteen beds in all. At one end of the room was the nurses' station, and at the other were a large TV and a room beyond that – the playroom. This was a room full of mainly broken donated toys and books. But it turned out there were actually quite a few fun things in there too. In particular, I discovered there were a lot of nice art materials; sheets and sheets of lovely cartridge paper, tissue paper and sugar paper in all different colours. There were pens, pencils, crayons and pastels and lots of white glue.

School, Vicky and the other bullies were now forgotten in my new adventure with illness. Every morning a lady, Mrs Sykes, would come in to hold a sort of informal teaching session in the playroom for those children who were up and out of bed and who could manage a bit of school work. Mrs Sykes was quite old and I suspect she was a retired teacher, who perhaps wasn't even paid for her time with us. For two hours she would sit with five or six of us, all different ages, and try and get us to write stories or letters. Sometimes she attempted a bit of maths teaching. But she was very soft and had no natural authority. We children usually managed to steer the lessons toward drawing, painting or making things. I showed Mrs Sykes how to make corn dollies using paper straws and we managed to wangle a whole week of doing nothing but making hundreds of white paper corn dollies using a huge bag of straws we found in the art supplies. We did run rings around Mrs Sykes but we loved her too.

At one point, a huge card arrived for me. It was from school, from all my classmates. A big get-well card, signed by every one of them. Even Vicky's signature was there – small and sheepish-looking, on a corner of the card.

'Oh, that's lovely!' said the nurse as I opened it. 'You must have loads of friends.' She took the card and stood it on the bedside cabinet. But as soon as she left I took it down and packed it away in a bag. I didn't want to be reminded of my old life.

I had a new place now, new people who didn't know the old me. New friends. I could talk to the other children in the ward and hear their stories. They took the place of my brother and sister, and became almost like my new family. I sadly don't remember many of their names. There were two children there with their legs wrapped up and suspended in the air. Although it looked like both were suffering with the same thing, I later found out that one had spina bifida, while the other, a little boy called Terry, fell out of his window and broke both legs while looking for Father Christmas. Most of the children on the ward were little ones, much younger than I was. But there was also an older teenage girl called Julie who was around sixteen or seventeen. Julie looked terribly ill and was all bandaged up in bed. She had been riding her horse when a motorbike roared past them. The horse had thrown her into the path of a car and she had been smashed to bits. Julie and a few other children had big signs on the head of their bed saying 'NIL BY MOUTH'. Apparently, this means that person is not allowed to eat anything because they are on a drip and are getting all their nutrients that way. I always wondered why they didn't just have a sign that said 'No food' or 'No eating'. It would have been far less confusing.

I don't even remember missing my family or my home, not at all. But there was good reason for that: my mother came in every single day to see me. *Every day!* Even though it was a thirty-mile drive to the hospital and she had my sister and little brother to cope with too. Sometimes Dad came, usually at the weekends as he often worked too late to come in the week. He always brought me comics that were too young for me. I wanted *Just 17* but he usually brought me the *Beano* and the *Beezer*. I didn't really mind.

In the children's ward there were no visiting hours. Parents were allowed to visit any time, staying all day if they wanted. I would often chat to the other parents and proudly tell them, 'I have temporal lobe epilepsy'. It just sounded so cool and important to have such a condition and I wore this identity like a badge of honour. It seemed so much more impressive than some of the less medical-sounding conditions, like glue ear and asthma.

Every day my temperature would be taken, my eyes were checked and my tablets were brought to me in a little plastic cup. Often, I was given a blood test. On one day I was given four blood tests, one out of each arm and one out of each hand. I went around for the next few days with four little round plasters covering each needle hole. I felt tremendously proud of these. It felt like a sort of honour to be given so many blood tests and to have coped so bravely.

If I was bored in the afternoons, I would ask the nurses if they needed any help. Not all the nurses were friendly but I got to know the more approachable ones and befriended them. Some of them would let me carry things as they did their checks. They would send me with a message to ask this or that child if they needed a drink, or whether they needed the toilet. I would be asked to stack things, or to count the little bottles for urine tests. Sometimes the littler children would cry when their parents left in the evening and I would offer to read them a story.

I know now that the nurses were probably only humouring me, giving me things to do to occupy me, perhaps even to keep me out of the way sometimes. But at the time I truly felt indispensible. I had made myself so useful I felt sure the nurses couldn't now do without me. I was important, loved, an essential part of the running of the ward. It must have been noticed how helpful I was. I felt sure there were conversations happening to discuss my future career at the hospital. I even had fantasies that one day, someone important would come in to the ward and take me aside to give me some news.

Siobhan, we've all noticed how helpful you've been around here. And we've decided we can't do without you. We've decided to offer you a job as a nurse and you can live in the hospital.

I ran through this over and over in my mind. I was sure someone would notice just how much I wanted to be there and how essential I was to the working of this hospital.

Maybe I would never have to go to school again. I would never leave this new life. I would live here, on the ward forever.

I remember years later watching a TV science programme about brainwaves and EEGs, something like *Horizon* or *Tomorrow's World*. I remember it clearly. The narrator said that when looking at EEGs, everyone's brainwaves are quite different and variable. But there is one clear pattern that is unmistakeable in every single case – *the spike.* This particular spike in brainwaves was absolute and unmistakeable proof of epilepsy. And this makes the EEG diagnosis of epilepsy one of the most reliable and clear tests in all of medicine.

What complete rubbish!

It's perfectly possible to fake that test. I know, because I did it. I went on to have maybe half a dozen EEGs, and every one apparently confirmed my status as an epileptic. I received many more drugs including Epilim, a drug suspected by some to cause birth defects and that has been at the centre of a huge court case.

But I never once had a true symptom of epilepsy. I never felt dizzy. I never fainted. I never 'spaced out'. I certainly never had a fit.

It was all fake.

You know, it has crossed my mind this very moment as I write these words that I *did* have a sort of illness. It just wasn't epilepsy. I had some sort of childhood Munchausen Syndrome, brought on by the stress of extreme bullying and a strong instinct for survival.

CHAPTER 14

I spent an entire month in hospital. I know these days people are chucked out of hospital hours after having operations, but back then, long stays in hospital were commonplace. There just seemed to be no rush whatsoever to get me home. The attitude seemed to be: if in doubt, stay in another week.

My big, big mistake was in becoming complacent. I had come to love being in hospital so much that I ended up forgetting about my own illness. I was supposed to be ill. I was not to be having a good time. And the truth was, I forgot to continue faking it.

I was a bright and breezy part of the gang. I was everyone's friend, the nurses' helper. To onlookers, it was clear the new drug combination was helping enormously and that I was getting much better. What no one realised was that very often I didn't even take the pills. Sometimes they would stick in my throat and make me choke on their horrible taste. I also think they upset my tummy sometimes. So most of the time, I just took them from the nurse, pretended to put them in my mouth and then swallowed the little bit of water they gave me. I would then pop the pills into the overflow of the basin while washing my hands. I'm sure I felt better without them.

Then the day finally came. A nurse came in to tell me the 'good' news.

'Guess what, Siobhan? You're going home tomorrow! Isn't that great?'

What? Home? No! I couldn't. I couldn't return. This was my home now. I belonged here. I was accepted here. They *needed me.* Everyone loved me. I couldn't go home. I just couldn't.

I couldn't go back to school. How could I *possibly* go back to school? Back to the bullies? Back to *Vicky?*

When the nurse left, I went to the toilets and cried. I was going to have to say goodbye to my friends, to my hospital home, to my *life* here. This wonderful little world was going to be disappearing from my life and I might *never* see it again. Everything was coming crashing down. I would return to the previous hell I had been living. It was like a nightmare.

And all too soon, I was in the car on the way home, having said a few goodbyes to the ward. I had expected some sort of leaving party or a ceremony to mark my leaving, but there was no occasion at all. The nurses I had thought valued me so much just waved goodbye, almost in passing, as if I was just like any other ordinary patient on the ward. No one had come to offer me a job in the hospital, like in my fantasy.

I don't even remember what my mum said on the trip back, or whether she was pleased to have me home. I just remember the sinking feeling of dread as we drove past the school on the way to our house. I clearly remember going straight to my room, and throwing myself onto the bed. Compared to the hard, high hospital bed, my soft bouncy mattress felt like a squashy cloud and I felt as if I was falling right through it. My bedspread felt like fluffy down compared with the starched white hospital bedding I had become used to. This was no comfort and I longed to be back on the ward where I was safe.

And, horror of horrors, I was expected to go back to school tomorrow, *the very next day!* No easing in gently. No day to recover and prepare myself. *The very next day.*

How... *how* could this be happening?

Next morning, I could think of no more excuses for staying home. Mum drove me to school and I was brought into class by the teacher, reintroduced to the class, just like the way they would with a new kid.

'Siobhan's back,' said Mr Batts. 'She's been very ill so I want you to be extra kind to her for a bit.'

As if.

Vicky was looking at me calmly across the room. There was nothing in her eyes to give away what she was thinking. I wondered what she was plotting. Perhaps she was still trying to assess the situation. What do you do with a child who has just come home from a month in hospital? Are the rules still the same? I do remember standing there and wondering if things would be different now.

In my school, it seemed that certain types of illness provoked sympathetic, interested, even envious reactions. A broken leg in a cast, for example, was likely to inspire a lot of attention. Surgery too. If someone had an operation and had a scar or stitches – that was a thing of great fascination for one's classmates, like battle wounds. Everyone wanted to be near this person and was proud to know them. Children with operation scars became heroes for the day.

But those illnesses that seemed to have no obvious *visible* mark, no sign or proof – flu, glandular fever, epilepsy – these were not interesting at all. In fact, these conditions were more likely to elicit disdainful or even disgusted reactions. Those off school having surgery were treated as fascinating heroes. Those off school with invisible illnesses were treated more like lepers. I have never really understood why.

So, as I stood in front of the class, they were initially somewhat enthralled by me. They wanted to know all the gory details.

'Did you have an operation?'

'Have you got stitches?'

'What was wrong with her, Sir?'

And then, the ever-clueless Mr Batts, with his infinite stupidity, said something that would make my life immeasurably worse.

'Siobhan just has a brain disease called epilepsy,' he said with attempted kindness. 'It's nothing to be scared of. Siobhan doesn't have anything wrong with her body. She just has something wrong with her mind.'

Sniggers burst out. Now the children, and especially Vicky, knew the rules about how to treat this particular invalid. Mr Batts had just helped them understand. I had something wrong with my *mind*. I had epilepsy, and a lot of them knew about epilepsy. That was the disease that made you fall on the floor and shake and foam at the mouth.

I looked at Vicky. She was half smiling now, as if to say, 'Oh, what fun this is going to be!'

CHAPTER 15

The kids did go easy on me for a few days. They tiptoed around a little, just asking questions. There were a few 'eppie' jokes and I could handle those. But within a week or so, the hesitancy had worn off.

And what fun Vicky had with my epilepsy. It began in the class one morning before registration when someone asked me out loud, 'What *is* epilepsy?'

That was Vicky's cue. 'I'll show you,' she said. She then proceeded to fall to the floor and begin kicking and shaking, faking the most violent seizure, convulsing her body in great kicking shudders. The whole class leapt to its feet to watch.

Vicky's tongue was poking out and she made a terrible moaning, shrieking noise like you might hear from a very disturbed mentally ill person. Finally, she made a puking noise, to imitate the foaming at the mouth that every epileptic person, of course, suffers with.

The class was now shrieking with laughter. Even the kinder children smiled at Vicky's performance. Vicky truly was a very funny person. It was part of her charm and power. If only her comedy hadn't always been at someone else's expense.

Abruptly, the convulsions stopped. The class quietened as Vicky got to her feet, brushed herself off, and with impeccable comic timing said to the waiting crowd,

'*That's* epilepsy!'

The class erupted with clapping and congratulations for Vicky's fine enactment. What charisma she had. I had to begrudgingly admire her. Even *I* somehow wished I could be Vicky's friend at that moment.

Over the next few days there were a few more 'on the floor' performances demanded of Vicky, just to repeat the act for those who missed out the first time. But soon she replaced the falling on the floor act with simply shaking and convulsing in her chair whenever I looked her way. Sometimes the other members of her gang, usually Sam, Emma and Sharon would, in unison, launch into the same shaking fit in their chairs when I entered the room.

'Throwing an eppie' became a way of describing anyone losing their temper or getting angry or irritated. 'Okay, okay, don't throw an eppie!' would be the response to anyone, child or milder teacher, who showed any form of heightened emotion.

The bullying was now worse than ever.

CHAPTER 16

Does it sound like I talk of nothing but myself? Do I sound a little self-obsessed? If it sounds like I thought only of myself, that's because I *was* thinking of myself most of the time. I was thinking of how to get through the week, the day, the next hour. I was thinking of what would happen next time I entered a room. I was thinking of new places to hide during break times. When your main aim is survival, your focus does tend to become a little self-centred. I wish I *had* had the headspace to think of someone else, something else, *anything* else. But most of the time, I just didn't.

There were a lot of cruel kids in my school, there were some that physically hit and scratched, or pulled hair or pushed me to the ground, some stole and hid my belongings, some just called me vile names or told me I stank. But Vicky's bullying began to take a very particular form. She had an oddly sexual element to her bullying. She would unwrap condoms (or 'rubber johnnies' as we called them) or save used tampons and leave them inside my desk. She would also draw pencil drawings of me (she was an excellent artist) naked but with a huge, impossibly enormous penis. She would tape these to the blackboard or to the underside of my desk lid. More than once she and her cronies, Sam, Emma and Sharon, followed me into the girls' toilets to stand on the toilet in the adjoining cubicle and torment me as I urinated. They would shout and throw toilet paper on me as I sat there. Vicky would shout,

'I can smell your piss from here, you dirty bitch.'

'I can see your hairy fanny – you're disgusting.'

'Ughhh! Look, she's playing with herself. She's having a fit and playing with herself!'

Looking back, it does cross my mind that Vicky probably had quite a disturbed mind. I have often wondered whether she herself was a victim of sexual assault. At the very least, she seemed overly sexualised for a thirteen-year-old.

Of course, I'm not stupid. I know that *all* children giggle and snigger at sex and bodily functions, and teenagers can find sexual innuendoes in the most innocent of comments and situations. But Vicky's sexualisation was extreme, even becoming violent. On several occasions she and her friends chased me into a corner on the playing field during lunch break and stripped me naked. This Vicky called 'rape' although what it actually entailed was their tearing off my clothes and throwing them into the hedge. They would then leave me to retrieve my clothes as they ran laughing back to school.

But Vicky's weird sexual attacks were starting to go too far. After one 'rape', Vicky held me down and suggested they check to see if I had a tampon in. This was the final straw for one girl, Emma.

'Aw, that's gross. That's enough, Vick. She's had enough, leave her alone now.'

Emma didn't walk back with Vicky and the other girls, she picked my clothes out of the hedge, stayed to help me get dressed and walked back with me. She didn't talk about it or apologise. She didn't need to. It was enough that she was there. I knew that staying back to help me was a form of apology. Emma seemed to distance herself from Vicky after that and eventually extricated herself from the gang completely. Ironically, she would, in time, go on to become a good friend of mine.

The bullying went on over almost my entire time at secondary school. When I felt really under pressure from Vicky I would fake a fainting spell. A faint was a guaranteed instant way of stopping whatever was going on and getting a lift home to spend a couple of days with Mum. I had quite a few more single days away from school and even a few full weeks. In time, even Mum's sympathy seemed to wane just a little and she became less likely to allow me just to take time away from school whenever I felt like it. So I couldn't overdo it. I couldn't go fainting every day only and whenever Vicky was around, and I never did return to the wonderful fantasy time of that first spell of faked illness. Illness was no longer the powerful tool it once was for me.

CHAPTER 17

I'd like to say that everything changed when the other girls had a spontaneous change of heart, or that I found my inner mental confidence, grew in character, became strong and found a way to stand up to the bullies. I wish that were true. Sorry to disappoint you but the truth is far more mundane.

We were just teenage girls, remember? And teenagers are shallow. It was at the age of 14 that I had my first perm. It was the '80s – the time of 'big hair', and permanent waves were all the rage. At least half the class already had one. Even a couple of the boys had experimented with them, although they weren't so successful and usually ended up being chopped off shortly after. Like most perms, mine started off super curly, sticking straight up from my head like a huge Afro. I knew I would be tormented for my silly hair the moment I walked into the class. I was dreading it so much I actually faked a couple of sick days, so terrified was I to face the reactions of the class.

When I finally walked into the class the first morning of sporting my new look, Vicky took one look at me and literally *screamed.*

'Errrrr! Your hair looks like *puke!'*

This was followed by hysterical forced laughter as she pointed and doubled up in her screeching mirth at my extremely normal-looking new hairdo.

But that perm signalled a change in me. After a few weeks, as always happens, the curl dropped a bit, leaving long, delightfully curly hair. Copying a look I had seen on *Grange Hill,* I tied a ribbon around my head, like an Alice band.

'Your hair looks lovely,' said Jacky, one of the kinder girls.

'No it bloody doesn't,' said Vicky. 'She looks like a freak.'

But Jacky wasn't one to be easily led. She seemed to warm to me and we became friends. She even asked me to stay over at her house one Friday evening. We spent the evening chatting and putting on make-up. I *loved* that evening. I felt for the first time like a normal girl, like a teenage girl.

'Your eyes look *so* pretty with mascara on,' she said. 'It really suits you.' And that was when I first looked in the mirror and saw looking back at me, not a freak or an ugly monster, but really quite a pretty face. I liked what I saw.

With newfound confidence, I started wearing a bit of make-up to school every day. I'm sure it was just the change in my appearance that made people start to like me. I know it was not that they had grown up and matured. I knew that they were just responding well to my improved looks. But I didn't care; I still loved it.

I became part of a group again. Not the most popular, Vicky-led group, obviously, but one of the lesser, more academic, slightly peripheral groups. We didn't talk about sex and smoking and who was going out with whom. We talked about horses, television, Boy George and Tony Hadley. We weren't cool, far from it. We were what would now be called nerds or geeks. But it was fun. The girls were kind. And I was happy at school for the first time ever.

And so, I am convinced that it was by becoming just a little more physically attractive that the wind began finally to change for me.

I remember one morning in the fourth year when we were preparing for our yearly class photo. We had all congregated in the library where the photo was to be taken against an academic-looking backdrop of shelves and shelves of books.

The photographer asked us to stand in a line according to height, from shortest to tallest, so that he could arrange us nicely for the photograph. I was astonished to discover that, without my noticing, almost all of the girls and all of the boys had caught up with me in height. I looked around and realised I was no longer the tallest in the class. In fact, I was somehow now the second shortest.

This seemingly insignificant event had a huge effect on me. Inside, I was still a mouse. But my *physical* confidence increased dramatically. I was no longer the tall, gangly, gauche one in the class chosen to carry the heavy gym kit. My early-developed breasts weren't even particularly big any more compared to the rest of the class. In fact, they were on the small side.

I felt little, like a pixie. I could strut about with my head held high and not look like an awkward freak. I could be small, girlish, perhaps even cute.

My growth spurt had been very early, but actually not very extreme, it seems. Because I never really grew again after that. I have remained short in height and fairly flat-chested my entire life. And I now love being that way.

Anyway, back to the story.

It was shortly after this that the unthinkable happened. A boy asked me out.

It was at a town event, a church fete or a jumble sale, that I met up with Geoffrey. He was a boy from my own class. He had never shown me any attention whatsoever at school, but here, away from his usual peer group, I was the only familiar face in a crowd of strangers, and so we began chatting. He was a nice, kind boy and made me laugh a lot. There was no element of tough-guy or machismo with Geoffrey. Eventually, Jacky joined us and the three of us ended up hanging around together for the entire day. We laughed, and joked around and had the best time. It was one of the happiest days of my childhood. When Jacky went home, Geoffrey walked home with me and we chatted all the way. It was so easy to talk to him and we never ran out of things to say. When we reached my house and it was time to part, Geoffrey asked if I would like to meet him tomorrow – Sunday – to go to town and buy a record he wanted. We could get some chips and mess about, he suggested.

So that Sunday, I spent an entire day alone with Geoffrey, looking at music, eating chips, sitting in Poppins café drinking tea and having a wonderful time. As teenagers, we would only drink tea in places that gave an extra jug of hot water alongside the teapot. Poppins was one of those cafés deemed worthy of our patronage. Once the teapot was topped up with hot water, we could often eke out four or five cups of tea each. For the price of a cup of tea, we could sit and drink for hours in a café. This meant a lot to children whose money is scarce and pennies matter.

Geoffrey paid for two jam doughnuts to go with our tea. I knew he was only being friendly. I knew we were just 'mates' but that didn't matter. He was genuinely enjoying my company and that was more than enough.

Things move quickly when you are a child and it was at school a few days later that a message came to me, via another girl, acting as go-between.

'Geoffrey wants to know: Will you go out with him?'

Jacky gasped and gave me a big nudge. Geoffrey was not just friendly and funny and easy to talk to, he was also one of the cool kids in the class. He had 'been out' with lots of girls before and half the class fancied him. But there was more than that. This wasn't just any old Geoffrey. It was Geoffrey *Simpson* – this was Vicky's younger brother.

Of course, I had to say 'yes'. This was the biggest moment of my school life so far. It was an honour, my moment in the sun. And following a suitable response to the go-between, I, Siobhan Lennon – the spastic, the flid, the ugly freak – was now going out with Vicky Simpson's brother.

CHAPTER 18

To say Vicky was upset by this turn of events would be something of an understatement, and by the end of that same day I got to learn her feelings in no uncertain terms.

'Vicky's gonna kill you!' I heard from one source.

'She's gonna get you after school,' from another.

By carefully planned exits, lifts from my mother and a few other avoidance plans, I managed to escape Vicky's attacks for a few days. But she would look across the classroom at me and mouth 'I'm gonna get you, bitch!'

It was close to the end of the Christmas term. I knew I only had a few weeks to get through before I would be free and safe for the whole Christmas holiday. It was after a school disco that it happened. We, like most other secondary schools, would hold a school disco at the end of every term. These discos were massively important social events for us back then. They were the chance to forget the school uniform, dress up in our new, fashionable clothes, wear lots of make-up and do our hair. They were the chance to catch the eye of the boy we fancied, perhaps have a dance and even a quick snog in the shadows.

And this time, it was special. This time, I was going to the disco as the proud girlfriend of Geoffrey Simpson. I knew Vicky would be there. But I wasn't going to miss this disco for anything.

I turned up at the disco wearing a new ruffled skirt and a white frilly blouse. I had a blue satin ribbon in my hair that I thought matched the colour of my eyes. Fashion was heavy on frills and ribbons at the time. There was a lot of colour and satin. The New Romantics were very big then and we girls idolised them with their flamboyant style. Jacky and some other girls immediately joined me and we stood in an excited huddle, complimenting each other's clothes and make-up.

But I could see Vicky and her cronies across the hall, eyeing me with hatred. Above the noise, I heard Vicky's voice.

'I said, "I'm gonna get that bitch!"'

'Oh, don't listen to her. She's just pissed off because of Geoffrey,' said Jacky kindly. 'She can't touch you now.'

Was that really true? Was I untouchable now that I was going out with her brother? This really was going to be a magical night. Or so I thought...

We girls went into the big assembly hall to join the disco. Geoffrey was in there already, standing against the wall with some other boys. On seeing me, he came straight over and said 'hi'. I could tell he was a bit embarrassed and shy, a bit nonchalant like a typical teenage boy, but I was thrilled to see him. I had barely spoken to him since he asked me out, other than a few awkward words in the corridor and the odd smile. I remember he was wearing light grey trousers and a pale blue leather tie. I thought he looked amazing. I felt so proud to be there with him – one of the coolest boys in the year, going out with *me*.

The three of us, Geoffrey, Jacky and I, had a few nervous, awkward dances and then just stood around chatting. I noticed that whenever Vicky came near, Geoffrey would lead me away, with the pretence of getting a drink, or saying he needed to cool down. I don't know what they had discussed, I don't know what she had told him but it was clear that he was doing his best to stay out of her way.

At the end of the night, the DJ played 'True' by Spandau Ballet and Geoffrey and I had a close dance together. I put my arms around his neck, like I had seen in films, and he put his arms around my waist. It felt like I was dancing at a royal ball or a red carpet event in Hollywood.

Vicky stood and glowered from the side of the room. She really did have no power here. No one had asked her to dance and her own brother had no time for her. Apart from her little group of four, no one was paying the slightest bit of attention to her.

Geoffrey and Vicky had always been very close until now. They had always walked to school and home together. And even if they didn't spend every lunch break together, they were always obviously happy in each other's company – more like great friends than brother and sister. I almost felt the tiniest bit sorry for Vicky as he shunned her company so obviously and publicly.

But I think what made Vicky snap properly, to lose it big time, was that it looked, quite plainly, that he was rejecting her for *me*, for the epileptic freak. For Vicky Simpson, a leader all her life, I think the shame of that was just too much.

She wasn't going to stand for it any longer. She was about to take drastic action – action that would have terrible repercussions for both of us.

It was at the end of the evening when it happened. I had said my goodbyes to Geoffrey and walked off with Jacky to the top of the road to wait for my dad to pick me up in the car. I stood with Jacky, chatting as we waited for our lifts. Her dad drove up first, she got in and I waved as they pulled away.

I was standing alone on the pavement next to the top entrance to the school. There were still plenty of children milling around, some walking home, some saying goodbye, some waiting for lifts. I saw a group coming up the path toward me. In the darkness I couldn't recognise their faces but as they approached I heard the unmistakeable tones of Vicky.

'Told you she was up here,' Sam proudly announced, as if there was some twisted honour in being the one to tell Vicky the location of her intended victim. They all crowded round me with Vicky in front. Her face was like thunder, her huge mouth pursed together, pressing her thick lips in a tight line. I remember thinking how ugly she looked when she scowled like that. Vicky gave me a huge shove in the chest that nearly knocked me over before she spoke.

'Who the *fuck* do you think you are?' she said through gritted teeth. 'You think you're something now, don't you? You're not. You're just a fucking *freak.*'

'Leave me alone, Vicky, I'm not bothering you. I don't want to piss you off. Why can't you just leave me alone?' I didn't usually answer her back, but recently, and especially tonight, I had found the courage to stick up for myself a bit more.

But Vicky wasn't listening anyway. She manhandled me back into the school grounds, onto the grass and against the high hedge. It was a favourite spot for smokers and snoggers. The teachers rarely bothered patrolling as far away from the school building as up here.

'You want to fuck my brother, do you?' she spat. 'You think he'd fuck a slag like you? No one would fuck you. They'd only catch something, or die of being sick.'

'But... Geoffrey was the one that asked *me* out!' I said indignantly. 'And it's up to *him* who he goes out with.'

Vicky looked at me, astonished. It was the first time I had really stood up to her.

'Who do you think you're talking to, Freak? You want a *fuck,* do you? I'll give you a *fuck, you slag!*'

And then it happened. It's so hard for me to write what I am about to say. The remainder of this chapter took me months to complete because even now the memory is traumatic for me.

Vicky pushed me to the ground and the other girls automatically helped to hold me down.

'Right, let's see if she's still got that big hairy cunt,' Vicky said, and she started to pull down my pants. One of the other girls, Judith Watson, let go of the arm she was holding down that allowed me briefly to fight back.

'What you doing, Vick?' she was clearly shocked.

But Vicky took my spare hand and knelt on it, making me scream. The others were still holding me down, sitting and leaning on my legs to stop me kicking.

'I'll give you a fuck, you fuck! Keep holding her,' she ordered. And Vicky then rummaged in her own bag and brought out a round, narrow, cream-coloured hairbrush. Realising what she was about to do, I tried to clamp my legs shut but there were girls holding them fast. Vicky managed to get her hand and the brush between my legs. And holding it by the handle, she pushed the bristled end of the brush inside me. The scratching pain of the sharp bristles felt like needles. I screamed out loud, but a hand was immediately clamped over my mouth to muffle the noise. I thought she must have cut me open, the pain was so intense.

'Vick, *stop it!'* yelled Judith. And then to the other girls she said, 'Get off her! Vick's gone mad!'

Suddenly, as if they had only just realised what was going on, they all loosened their grip on me, and almost in unison, all the girls but Vicky let go of my arms and legs. They stood up and looked at each other, horrified. I knew they were all shocked at what had just happened.

'Vick, you can't do *that!*' said someone. There was a movement of girls toward me and the brush was removed with a yank and, I think, thrown out of sight.

Only Vicky stayed on the ground, trying still to hold me down. She had managed to manoeuvre herself so that she was now sitting on my chest and had hold of my hair. She started beating me about the face, slapping, punching as I tried to fend her off with one hand that I had managed to get free. She was like some sort of crazy thing. The fury of her jealousy over Geoffrey and her pure hatred of me and my oddness poured out of her and into her fists. She looked deranged, like she had lost her mind.

There was only one thing I could do. I had only one source of power. Almost without thinking, I started to shake and convulse. I began to throw the fake fit of all fits, the mother of all pretend seizures, giving Vicky exactly what she had wanted to see all this time. I kicked violently. I made my teeth chatter and made a strange humming noise. I began to moan in an unearthly way. I don't know what I was doing. I wasn't even thinking. I just had to get her off me.

But my throwing an apparent fit only seemed to anger her more. She stopped slapping me and put both her hands around my neck. She began to squeeze.

And then, a miracle happened. The other girls turned on Vicky.

'Vick, get off her, you freak!'

'What's wrong with you?'

'Leave her alone.'

'Fuck, she's gone mad.'

'Help me pull her off.'

Between them, the other girls pulled Vicky off me and dragged her, spitting venom, away from me. One of them came over to me and knelt down.

'Siobhan, you okay?' I opened my eyes. It was Sam, the biggest, toughest girl, Vicky's 'muscle'. She looked at me with big, wide brown eyes; it looked like she was going to cry.

'Go, Siobhan, go now!' she said.

I stumbled away from them and walked to the top of the road. My dad was already waiting in the car.

'You've been ages?' he said. 'Where were you?'

'Saying goodbye to people,' I mumbled.

'Did you have a good time?' he asked.

'It was alright,' I shrugged. I'm glad it was Dad picking me up. Mum would have noticed something was wrong and probed me to get the details. But Dad was happy to drive home in silence.

On arriving home, I went straight inside and up to my room without saying a word to my mum.

'Siobhan, you okay, my love?' Mum called up the steps.

'Yes, Mum. Just a bit knackered out,' I replied with as normal a voice as I could.

I could feel a burning feeling down below, like a singing pain between my legs. When I checked I was surprised to see no blood. I was just badly scratched. But I was grazed and bruised everywhere and one of my hands was cut and bleeding. There were bits of gravel and dirt stuck in the cuts. I rinsed my hand in the bedroom basin, dried myself off and sat on the end of the bed.

That's when the horror of what had happened hit me. What she had done to me, the depth of her hatred and the viciousness of her attack. And I wept. My body tried to sob but I didn't want my mum to hear me crying. So I cried silently, my body shuddering and shaking in my attempts to contain the noise until I finally fell asleep.

CHAPTER 19

The next day was Saturday. I spent the whole weekend trying to think up reasons not to go to school on Monday. I even thought of running away from home. But Monday morning came and I had no better plan than to try and fake another illness. But this time, Mum wasn't having any of it.

'You're not ill, Siobhan. You just don't want to go to school. Come on, now. Get yourself dressed.'

'But, Mum, I really can't go in today. Please don't make me.' I started to cry. Then Mum knew something was really wrong.

'What is it, Siobhan?' Mum looked worried. 'What's wrong?'

My mum was such a kind lady. She did everything for me and she sometimes would cry when my little brother cried. She couldn't stand to see us sad. I really didn't want to tell her the story because I knew it would upset her so much. It would have killed me to see my mum cry again because of me. But I needed to say something.

'Mum, it's that girl at school who picks on me. She...she beat me up on Thursday after the disco.' I showed her the cuts on my hand and several big bruises on my legs. 'It was really horrible. I thought she was going to kill me, and I'm so scared to go to school now.'

'But the teachers all said they would make sure she left you alone now!' she said.

'I know. But they don't know what she's really like. They think she's trying hard. But she just waits until no one can see and then she's really horrible again, Mum.' I didn't care if Mum cried or not. I needed her to know.

'Please help me, Mum!' I whispered.

Mum took me into school herself and went with me straight up to the headmaster's office. I walked through the corridor looking at the floor, blocking out the noise of other children. But as we approached his door, it opened and he started to walk out.

'Ah, Siobhan, and your mother. I'm glad you're here. Come in, come in.' It was like he was expecting us.

'Siobhan,' he told me when we were sitting down inside. 'Some of the other girls have told me about what happened on Thursday at the disco. I'm sorry, Siobhan. Vicky will be punished properly this time.'

As the conversation went on, it was clear that the other girls had not told the full story about the hairbrush. They knew what that would have done to me. It was an unspoken, unacknowledged but completely understood certainty that the adults didn't need to know about that particular detail. Remember, we were teenage girls and were easily embarrassed, shamed and humiliated. If the adults knew about the hairbrush incident all hell would have broken out. Investigations, police even. Everyone would know and that would make it far worse for me.

The hairbrush was never mentioned again, not by me, nor by any of the other girls. Instead, this had been reported as a simple case of bullying.

Maybe you can't understand this, but I was ever-grateful to the other girls for that.

The headmaster didn't really give Vicky a punishment that fitted her crime. She got a two-week suspension to begin after Christmas, she was on permanent report and was told to stay well away from me. If there was another incident, she would be expelled.

The scratches and cuts quickly healed. Physically, I wasn't really badly hurt. Emotionally, it was more serious. To this day, I can't look at one of those thin, round bristle brushes. You often find the round brushes in hairdressers but I only have the flat, paddle-type brushes at home. But I have also had a lot of confusion over the years about this incident. Because while it was a source of horror for years, something that haunted me and made my eyes prick with tears whenever I thought of it, that night was also the event that signalled everything changing immeasurably for the better in my life.

That Monday at school after the incident, only Sam was sitting with Vicky. Sam, the loyal, tough henchwoman was the only one still faithful. All of the rest of her posse had abandoned her. And while Sam was sitting next to her, she was looking around sheepishly at the class as if she didn't want to be with Vicky either. It would only be a few days before she, too, gave up the company of Vicky Simpson.

Geoffrey said *nothing*, like awkward, self-conscious teenage boys will tend to do. He didn't even look at me for ages. Our 'going out together' had died a death before it had even begun.

The girls in the class were whispering and tittering about Vicky. The story appeared to be going round that I had done 'one of my faints' and while unconscious, Vicky had tried to have sex with me. The story went on that Judith, Sam and Sharon had heroically had to pull her off so that I could escape. The hairbrush incident was never mentioned. I thank the girls for that.

CHAPTER 20

This was the end of the reign of Vicky Simpson as queen of the school. From that moment, Vicky was no longer cool. She was no longer funny and she was no longer able to command or lead the other children. It seemed the girls who witnessed the attack were disgusted, appalled and a bit creeped out by her. They treated her like she was scary and sick, like she was a pervert or a monster.

Vicky was now the weird one! She was now the freak.

And as these stronger, tougher girls like Sam and Sharon had turned on Vicky, the rest of the class naturally and effortlessly followed their lead, having nothing to do with Vicky any more. That same day we went into a French lesson and someone had written a message on the board.

'Vicky Simpson is a lezzy perv.'

So the amazing thing was that Vicky *did* receive a punishment befitting her crime and it was far worse than detention or expulsion from school, or police involvement. Vicky was sentenced to the humiliation of being rejected by her peers.

Everything seemed to have changed for me too. It felt as if there was a mass, unspoken class apology going on. Girls were soon fighting to sit with me, partly to ask what had happened to elicit some more juicy details, but also in genuine friendship.

'So what really happened?'

'I always wanted to be your friend, but Vicky wouldn't let me.'

'No one likes her now. Did she really try and have sex with you?'

'Everyone likes you now.'

'Do you think she's a proper lesbian?'

'Do you want to come to mine on Friday?'

For a brief period, 'Vicky' became a term of abuse. 'Err, you *Vicky*,' girls would call each other, especially if there was anything remotely sexual, especially lesbian sexual, about the content of the insult.

Of course, I know that it wasn't just the ferocity and perverted nature of Vicky's attack on me that led to this school-wide change of attitude toward her. I think it was just the final catalyst for a change that had been coming for some time. The truth was, I think the other children had had enough of Vicky and her nastiness. We were growing up, becoming young women and men. Some of us had part-time jobs and were looking to the future, to jobs and university. We weren't silly kids anymore and I think everyone had grown out of having to bolster their egos with bullying. We were quite simply bigger and better than this now. Only Vicky seemed to still have that need to be top dog, leader of the pack, and to prefer power and instilling fear, instead of genuinely being liked. I think the other children *wanted* an excuse to turn away from Vicky. They wanted a reason to topple her from her perch. I just gave them an easy way out.

Vicky did manage to gather a few friends over the next months. She carried on picking on other children, but only in a very minor way. I don't think her heart was in it any more. No one paid much attention to her in class and she became something of a loner, spending time only with a couple of close friends and not interacting much at all with the rest of the class.

Maybe, given time, she would have eventually regained her power and begun another reign of terror. But she never got the chance, at least, not at our school. After the summer holiday I returned to school to start the fifth and final year of school. We had a new form teacher, Miss Bateman. Vicky wasn't in registration.

'We have a new pupil today, Jason Lineham,' said Miss Bateman. 'Say hello to Jason everyone. Oh, and Vicky's left.'

Just like that. *Vicky's left!*

Vicky, my tormentor, and her brother Geoffrey, my one-time boyfriend, had left the school. I never knew why. It was a strange time to take a child out of school – in the final year before O Levels. So her parents must have had a good reason. I always assumed it had something to do with the attack and Vicky's subsequent rejection and unhappiness at school. I hoped so, anyway.

Now, the nightmare truly was over for good. I had one whole year left at school and Vicky would not be part of it in any way. I could enjoy my final year at school without fear of attack or bullying. I could really start the rest of my life, here and now.

Vicky would never again haunt the classrooms and corridors of our school, and the truth is, I don't think she was ever really missed. Vicky had, until now, always been a popular and funny girl, but she had also brought a sort of anxious energy to the school. Things had always felt tense with her around, not just for me, but for *everyone*. Without her, I think all the children just felt calmer and happier generally. Ironically, things felt more *normal* with her out of the picture.

CHAPTER 21

Things move on quickly at this time of life and it didn't take long before Vicky became largely forgotten, or at least she was not talked about. We just got on with a normal school year, and a normal life. I became great friends with Emma, one of Vicky's previous assistants, and even with big Sam. I remained friends with Jacky throughout my life.

The 'epilepsy' magically got better once I no longer had a need for it. I gave up pretending to be ill, faking faints and taking days off school. I had better things to do now. I wanted to get into the technical college to do A Levels and couldn't waste time sitting around at home watching telly with my mum.

I eventually stopped taking the pills of my own accord. I was only swallowing them occasionally anyway and they had begun to accumulate, bottles and bottles of them. I just stopped getting the prescription filled and Mum and Dad never really asked me why. Perhaps they had suspected by now that the illness was at least partly made up. I never went back to see the specialist and the whole business of my being an epileptic was almost forgotten.

I did well at the end-of-year exams, getting eight O Levels, all grade A-C. I got two A grades. This doesn't sound like a lot compared with today's GCSE results but it was enough to get me onto an A Level course. In time, I would go on to university and do very well.

I can't pretend everything was perfect in my life from that point on. I'm sad to say the attack on me took a long time to heal. Physically, I was fine within a week or so. But emotionally, it took a lot longer to come to terms with what happened that night.

The weirdly sexual element of Vicky's attack has been a source of massive confusion for me, and I think this confusion has stopped me being able to move on, to move past what happened. I hear of those who have suffered far greater traumas and worse attacks than I ever did. I hear about children who have been raped, sold, beaten and abused their entire lives. And because of this, I often feel I don't have the *right* to be bothered by what happened to me. I feel sometimes I am disrespecting those other little children who have suffered true nightmares, sometimes at the hands of their own fathers, or strangers. At least I always had a loving family.

I didn't even know what to call the attack. It wasn't 'rape', and it was carried out by another child, a girl. So did I even have a right to feel so bad about what happened? These are the sorts of confusing thoughts I would have constantly.

Over the years my thoughts have ranged from trying to dismiss the whole event from my mind – *it was nothing, it was only carried out by a girl, not like a rape, not anything really serious at all* – to feeling utter and complete revulsion and disgust. When these feelings overcome me, I will rush to wash furiously and to shave off all my pubic hair. Even today I have a problem allowing my pubic hair to grow. I try to see it as womanly and beautiful and natural but it just has too many unhappy connotations for me. I had a brief period in my late teens of self-harming by cutting my genitals with a knife to make them bleed.

Although it was certainly a sexual assault, I think what scarred me the most was the spite and pure hatred I felt from Vicky at that time. Was I actually so deeply unlikeable that I genuinely warranted that level of venom? And did everyone feel this way, secretly? Did others harbour the same hateful feelings, but they were just too polite to say anything? Did I even deserve to live if I was that loathsome? These are some of the thoughts that have haunted me over the years.

I didn't tell my mother the full extent of what happened during those school days. But I did tell her everything years later, in my twenties. I have also told a few counsellors all the details and my own doctor. My mother and doctor urged me to tell the police, to get Vicky properly punished. But I have always resisted this suggestion strongly. After all, what good would that have done? What good would it have done *me*, to state all those horrible details in a police statement, and then to either be disbelieved and ignored, or worse, to have to drag the whole thing through the courts? The result for me could only be further humiliation and stress.

And all for what? To put Vicky in prison? What good would that do?

Was it my duty to tell in order to protect future victims? I don't think so. It's not like she was going to spend the rest of her life attacking girls with hairbrushes.

And my life didn't go to wrack and ruin. As I said, I worked hard that last year of school, got some A levels at the technical college, and eventually went to university where I had a great time. I did okay and came out with a half decent degree. I even did a masters degree some years later.

I also found a wonderful, insightful therapist, Stephanie. She has helped me enormously to understand what happened, why it happened, and to begin forgetting the past. The bad memories of childhood have now faded to ghostly echoes and I am really quite happy in life. I now have my own family, a great social life, and things are going well for me.

I still feel guilty about what I did to worry my parents, in particular my mother. But my lies did nothing to damage our relationship. In fact, I feel I love her even more for the kindness she showed me. She was there for me, and now that she is elderly, I am there for her, and I will be till the day she dies.

It was only in the last ten years of my life that I turned my attention to writing books. I had always had a bit of a skill for writing essays and so found the whole business of book writing came quite naturally to me. I soon became able to support myself with my writing, and I was able to give up working for other people and just to concentrate on my writing career. I feel blessed that I am now able to live a relatively easy life, on my own terms and according to my own timetable.

It is Sunday night as I type these words, and I know that all over this country, all over the world, there are children dreading tomorrow morning, terrified at the prospect of going to school. And it's not just school that holds a danger any more. Because, bullying is still going on today, now, right at this moment. These days, children live in dread of looking at their mobile phones and Facebook, for fear of seeing vicious, threatening comments. They can't even feel safe in their own homes. This thought makes my blood boil and my heart break.

I always knew that if I ever wrote a book about my experiences of abuse, I would use those books to help other children who might be suffering. It was Sophie Jenkins, the joint author of *Dirty Little Dog,* who suggested making a contribution to the NSPCC for every book sold. I thought this a perfect plan. I write books in many different genres but every book I have helped to write about child abuse helps to raise money for the NSPCC. Every single month I make a donation, dependent on the number of books sold.

CHAPTER 22
EPILOGUE

One morning, years after I had published my first book, I had been invited to speak, and sign copies of my latest book at the local bookstore of my previous hometown. The whole family had since moved away to another area of the country so I was staying a night at The Grand Hotel. I remember leaving my room in the hotel, and coming down the stairs into the hotel reception area. I was dressed smartly and had done my hair. I had made a big effort to be immaculately groomed, feeling confident, head held high. Dressing smartly helped me to overcome my fear of public speaking. You could say I was dressed to kill.

A woman in overalls was crouching down, picking something out of the stair carpet. A cleaner. She was kneeling across almost the whole step and I had to step right over her to get by. This all seemed rather disrespectful, to just step over someone on the floor, so I turned to smile an apology at the woman.

And I looked straight into the eyes of Vicky Simpson.

'Right, Siobhan?' she said with instant recognition. Her voice was deep and gravelly, like she had spent a lifetime of smoking cigarettes and shouting.

Her eyes, always bulbous, were now greyish yellow and her teeth were brown. She had a few tattoos on her forearms, not professional images, just hand-scratched names and patterns, like those done with a bottle of Quink and a compass needle. She had two inches of grey roots showing at the parting of her hair. I was open-mouth astonished. She must have been around 38 years old but she looked old enough to be my mother.

Vicky Simpson, the bane and nemesis of my life, the source of such power and fear for so long, was crouching at my feet, dressed in a stained gingham overall, picking filth out of a stair carpet. The difference in our situations, our demeanours, our looks, our *lives* was screamingly obvious. She caught my eye only once after speaking to me and then looked away and went back to her work. I could feel her discomfort.

Now, I am *not* someone to look down on a person doing a menial or manual job. I did these sorts of jobs myself while at university. I believe in rights for workers, a fair minimum wage, and all that goes with it. But this was different. This was not a kindly, hardworking, salt-of-the-earth chambermaid who deserved my respect: this was *Vicky Simpson.*

For a short moment we weren't grown women, we were just kids again. And because this was Vicky Simpson, and because I wasn't thinking very maturely, I just stared amazed at her with the kind of disgusted pity that Frodo feels for Gollum in *Lord of the Rings.* She was pathetic, pitiful, but in a disgusting way. I felt sorry for her, but also wanted to step on her like a worm, to squash that pathetic weakness out of her. Of course, I should have risen above, been magnanimous. To judge her for her lowly position would have been no better than to do all the vile things she had done to me. Two wrongs don't make a right, and all that.

Bollocks! I loved it. I loved rubbing her nose in my success. I loved the power I suddenly had over her. I loved the ashamed and embarrassed look on her face.

How had *she* made such a mess of her life, while mine had been successful? She had tormented my childhood, terrorised me with unspeakable cruelty. I was the one who should have failed at life. But no, it was she, the abuser, the perpetrator, not the victim, who had fucked up her life. She had *no right* to fuck up her life. If I could make a go of it, after all I had been through, so could she. She had had all the power! It was *her duty* to succeed!

I eventually composed myself, stopped staring, closed my open mouth, and turned to walk away down the stairs.

'Nice to see you again, Vicky,' I said as I left.

Later, I felt a bit bad about the way I had behaved. At the time, I *had* enjoyed seeing her squirm, but that sick satisfaction was short lived and I started to feel a little guilty for acting so insensitively.

Only some time later did I realise the catharsis of what had actually happened. Very soon following the incident in the hotel, it became apparent that all that hate and resentment I had held onto for so many years had gone, *gone!* Vanished! Years of resentment, fear and bitterness had evaporated.

I now *felt sorry for Vicky Simpson.*

Years have gone by since the incident in the hotel and I have now fully forgiven Vicky for all she did to me. It was a long process and, at first, I did this not for her at all, but for me. It was important that I didn't let her have any more power over me, so that even the painful memories would lose their impact. Stephanie, my therapist, convinced me the easiest way to do this was to find a way to forgive. Stephanie was right.

But I have also come to understand that there is just a frightened child inside of her too. There always was. But whereas my child has grown up, Vicky's inner child is probably still lost and afraid. It really is true that people only do bad things because they are hurting inside. It's hard to accept for a lot of people, but forgiving those who have wronged you is not an act of weakness, it is the most empowering and liberating thing you can do for yourself.

Someone once said that holding onto resentment is like drinking poison and waiting for the other person to die. So if you were a victim of bullying I have this one simple piece of advice: Find a way to forgive your bullies, not for their sake, but for *yours*.

And set yourself free.

If you enjoyed this book, please check out

Dirty Little Dog: A Horrifying True Story of Child Abuse and the Little Girl Who Couldn't Tell a Soul

Another shocking childhood memoir
by Kate Skylark *with Sophie Jenkins*

Sophie Jenkins is living a happy life in the idyllic Dorset countryside when she meets Martin Brett, the man who will go on to abuse her and haunt her dreams for years to come. A momentary act of neglect leads to a horrible series of events that leaves her changed forever.

Badly let down by the adults entrusted to care for her, Sophie's life begins to spiral downwards.

However, Sophie's message is ultimately one of hope and empowerment. She is in the process of rebuilding her life when fate leads her to encounter her childhood attacker once again. The story ends with a truly shocking climax.

For every book sold or borrowed, a donation will be made to the NSPCC

Printed in Great Britain
by Amazon

64998198R00095